The Birth of a Father

The BIRTH of a FATHER

MARTIN
GREENBERG, M.D.

CONTINUUM
NEW YORK

1985
The Continuum Publishing Company
370 Lexington Avenue, New York, N.Y. 10017

Printed in the United States of America

Library of Congress Cataloging in Publication Data

Greenberg, Martin, 1941-
The birth of a father.

Bibliography: p.
1. Fathers—Psychology. 2. Father and child.
3. Child rearing. I. Title.
HQ756.G72 1985 306.8'742 85-17107
ISBN 0-8264-0362-X

To my friends Al Grodner and John Taylor
who are no longer here
yet will always remain with me.
To my parents.
To my wife, Claudia.
And to our children Jonathan and Jacob.

Contents

Acknowledgments

This book would not have been possible without the tireless effort and support of many. But truly it was the fathers themselves who shared with me their precious moments of joy at the birth of their babies and their experience of falling in love with their children thereafter to whom I owe a special debt of gratitude.

I wish also to express my appreciation to my mentors and teachers: To Peter Ostwald, M.D., teacher, supervisor, research advisor, colleague, and friend. It was through our daily discussions in a special research seminar that my ideas on fathering began to flower. To Harry Wilmer, M.D., a teacher and friend who has always encouraged me in my search for meaning, for truth, and is a living example of the creative spirit. And to Joseph Wheelwright, M.D., teacher and friend who kindled in me the importance of laughter and not taking oneself too seriously.

I also owe a special debt of gratitude to several individuals, now deceased, who encouraged me to look to the family, to reach out to the father! To John Lind, M.D., former chairman of the Department of Pediatrics, Karolinska Institute in Stockholm, Sweden, who as my research advisor, teacher, and friend always emphasized the importance of the father, his presence at the birth and thereafter in his child's development. To Edith Jackson, M.D., who at Yale University and at the University of Colorado was tireless in her efforts to humanize the hospital experience following birth and who by introducing Rooming-In brought the father back beside his wife and child throughout his wife's hospital stay. To Anna Freud who provided encouragement in my study of the father-baby bond. And to Margaret Mead who, although skeptical early on, of the father's importance, nevertheless provided valuable assistance and support and subsequently acknowledged the intense bond that fathers can potentially have with their children.

I also wish to express my gratitude to Tom Main, M.D., who as my research advisor in London encouraged me as I began my early research on "engrossment" or father bonding. To Norman Morris, M.D. at Charing Cross Hospital, London, who allowed me access to new fathers and who was always supportive and helpful in my work.

I also wish to express my thanks to Dr. J. Anthony Ambrose, a creative reseacher in infant behavior, whose comments, unique formulations, and support were particularly helpful. He was instrumental in arranging my entree into several London teaching hospitals on short notice, thus allowing me to complete my research.

I also wish to express my gratitude to Allan Wilson, M.D., a helpful consultant in child and family psychiatry; to Dr. Smythe, who allowed me access to new fathers at University College Hospital in London; and to David Panton, M.D., who not only allowed me access to new fathers at St. Mary's (Paddington) in London but also enlisted further crucial help from medical students under his guidance.

A number of others provided tireless efforts in typing this manuscript. I am grateful to Libby Hoffman, to Beverly Wake, and especially to Marilyn Van Antwerp who stuck it out with me through the many revisions and also provided helpful advice. I am also grateful to Bill Goff and the staff of the Scripps Institute of Oceanography library in La Jolla for allowing me the physical space to do my writing. To Ernest Herman, managing editor of the *American Journal of Orthopsychiatry,* whose suggestions were crucial to the final publication of this work. And to Mike Leach at The Continuum Publishing Company who has always been available with help and assistance and from the first time that he saw this manuscript, recognized the importance of this work.

I owe a great deal to all those who read the manuscript and/or gave me suggestions and advice. To Phyllis Pfeiffer, Bob Finkel, Ph.D., Abot Ben Sussen, Tom and Marilyn Elias, Mike Medavoy, Martin Stein, M.D., Diana Cohen, M.A., Alayne Yates, M.D., Doctor Mort and Marjorie Shaevitz, David Janowsky, M.D., Jim Clapp, Ph.D., Linda Allgeyer and Norm Levitt, Natasha Josefowitz, Ph.D., Tracy Hotchner, Hedda Nussbaum, Joyce Sunilla, Jack Sanford, Ph.D., Bill Van Ornum, Ph.D., and Merri Snow-Houdyshell as well as to Doctors Diana and Louis Everstein. I am especially indebted to Louis Everstein in my choice of a title. I am also indebted to Marlene Mathews, Tom Wallace, Peter Elias, M.D., Lanie Carter, Mary Wong, Ph.D., Doctor Ron and Chris Smith, Paul and Julie Shahele, Cynthia Martin, Ph.D., Jack Heinowitz, Ph.D., to Rachel, Allison, and Daniel Grodner, and especially to Sharon Grodner, Ph.D., who also provided constant support and encouragement as well as helping me find fathers willing to share their experiences following their children's births.

Others provided helpful support and encouragement along the way when I at times felt like abandoning ship. Norman Cousins encouraged me by emphasizing the importance of the concept of engrossment or father bonding and his own work on humor made a significant impact on me. Benjamin Spock, M.D., was always helpful and encouraging, and his book *Baby and Child Care* was an inspiration in my own efforts to reach out to fathers. Elaine Hillard, M.A., and Amy Chu Finkel were especially important to me in the early going when this book was just taking shape. Likewise Paul Brenner, M.D., encouraged me to see this project through and Bob Friedman was always available for support, advice and urged me to keep plugging away. And finally to Dominic Addario, M.D., I owe the inspiration for beginning this book. For it was he who encouraged me to tape record my thoughts and feelings after the birth of my first child and it was from this recorded diary that this work evolved.

I am grateful to Douglas Cazort, a friend and instructor in creative writing at the University of Southern California who spent many late nights with me on the phone as I bemoaned whether I could finish this project. His support and encouragement helped me through many a writer's block.

I am indebted to Fitzhugh Dodson, Ph.D., who made many valuable suggestions and was always encouraging and helpful over the years of my writing this book. His own books on *How to Parent* and *How to Father* were also an inspiration for me.

My children Jonathan and, later, Jacob were for me living examples of the magic of children and helped teach me personally about the power of the father-child bond.

To my wife, Claudia, I owe so much. Her guidance, her support, and her own creative relationship with our children taught me much about bonding and being a father.

And finally, I wish to thank my dear friend and editor, Jenny Gumpertz, who labored over this manuscript, providing support as well as helpful suggestions. She listened to my self-doubts and encouraged me to not give up. And in the process, she helped me, not only to complete this book but also to evolve as a writer. To her, I am supremely grateful.

To all of these people—I express my thanks. Without their help this book could not have been a reality.

The Birth of a Father

Introduction

This book represents a very personal experience for me. For some time, beginning in 1964 during my training in medical school, I have been interested in the relationship parents have with their newborn infants. Like other investigators, I focused primarily on the mother's experience. In 1965 I went to Sweden where, sponsored by a National Institute of Health fellowship, I began research on mothers "rooming-in" (residing in the same hospital room) with their newborns. And it was in Sweden that I first began to notice the intense involvement that fathers seemed to have in the entire birth process.

Then in 1970, during my psychiatry training, I was doing additional studies on early mother-infant relations at the University of California Medical Center in San Francisco. One day when I went in to talk to a mother who had just given birth at the university hospital, I found her husband present. I noted the loving, tender manner with which he handled the baby. I saw both the new father and the mother share in the joy of looking at the baby and touching its soft skin, gently exploring their newborn. The parents seemed utterly at peace with themselves and their infant. The father derived great pleasure from holding and fondling the baby and frequently stared at it, utterly transfixed. He asked me, "Do you want me to leave so you can talk to my wife?" But I asked him to stay.

I felt that an event of enormous significance was taking place before my very eyes—the emergence of a family. The infant had not only deeply affected the mother, but also the father. The experience with this new family made a strong impression on me.

I felt driven to understand more about the father-newborn relationship, a relationship that had been previously dismissed as inconsequential. While completing my psychiatry training in London in

1971, I conducted a scientific study that verified the powerful early impact of the newborn on the father. It was fascinating that the strength of that impact did not seem to depend on the father's class or culture. The fathers were simply smitten with their infants.

The excitement of these professional discoveries was enhanced by a personal turning point, my marriage at Chelsea Town Hall in London to Claudia, a lovely vibrant woman whom I had met two years earlier. She was full of the spark of life and had a wondrous sense of humor, with a joyous full-bodied laugh that caused people to turn their heads and smile. Perhaps what most attracted me to her was her keen sense of adventure; I think she interacted with the explorer in me.

Our honeymoon was a period of extended travel in Europe. Upon our return to the United States, I completed my active military service, working as a staff psychiatrist at the U.S. Naval Hospital in San Diego, California. It was at this time, in 1974, that our son was born. It was a time of transition in many ways, for not only was I now entering the new world of fatherhood but ten days after his birth I received my discharge from the navy.

I worked as a psychiatrist in private practice for a few months before departing with my little family to Zurich, Switzerland. There, in addition to completing my studies I also attempted to cope with the stresses and strains of being a new parent.

As a new father I felt preoccupied and absorbed in my own infant, buffeted by emotions and forces over which I had no control. My son had a powerful impact on me, and I found myself acutely sensitive to him as well as to what I imagined was expected of me as a father. What really shocked me was the realization that I had never completely understood parents until I became a parent myself.

The event of fatherhood is a momentous occurrence in the life cycle of a man. It inevitably triggers off strong emotions—emotions that are multifaceted and often tumultuous. Men are in many ways isolated, and they tend not to talk about their feelings. Discussions about their hopes and aspirations, their fears, joys, and concerns are not encouraged in our American culture. Men are supposed to be strong, solid, aggressive, assertive. They are certainly not supposed to be weak, passive, womanly, or maternal (whatever those terms mean). Frequently, and I might say unfortunately, our culture defines the expression of feelings as weakness. Even a man's joy in the experience of contact with his newborn infant is often seen as weakness, and even worse, as womanly and maternal. Clearly, such a narrow perspective hampers the new father from getting in touch with his true emotions.

This book is an attempt to break through that constricting environment. For it is a setting that creates an emotionless vacuum for the new father. I want to emphasize the importance of the human response—the far-reaching ramifications of the father's interaction with his newborn and the impact this has on his feelings about his infant, his wife, and perhaps most significantly about himself. The process of becoming a father is a gradually unfolding phenomenon, similar to the pregnancy but running on its own timetable. At times there is chaos, at times anger, and at times joy. But the process continues ever forward and in the end reaps a bountiful harvest. The birth of a child can be a process of reawakening for all fathers, increasing the breadth and depth with which we view the world.

•1•

Companionship: Union of the Spirits

I would like to tell you about the companionship that developed between my son Jonathan and me while he was still a little baby. The notion of a baby as a companion might at first seem amusing and even outlandish. A newborn is, after all, so small and dependent, always needing to be attended to and cared for. He is unable to speak and communicate. But is this really so? Doesn't that newborn reach out to us with his own unique language, a language so universal in its appeal that it goes beyond mere words? And isn't his presence frequently sufficient to unleash a flood of emotion and break down the walls that separate us not only from him but also from ourselves? Perhaps!

Well . . . let's see!

Viewing my infant son's birth was an overwhelming experience for me. But it was when he first began to smile, and shortly thereafter to coo, at around two months of age that I really felt he was beginning to respond to me as a person. As his face brightened when he saw me, I felt my own world light up. If I was feeling dejected and in the doldrums, his smile illuminated my mood and washed away the gloom. It compelled me to reach out to him, to hug and hold him. The realization that he was responding specifically to my face even at this early age was very exciting to me. It was at this point that our relationship became more and more a two-way stream, and our companionship began to grow and flourish.

I began taking Jonathan for strolls when he was very young. Using a modified baby sling, I carried him against my chest and abdomen until he was four months old and thereafter carried him on my shoulders in a backpack. Our walks together became treasured moments during which I shared my thoughts and feelings with him, a process that bound us ever closer together. Jonathan became my "confidant." I talked to him about things we saw—about the sky, the ocean, the trees, the birds. And I told him what I was feeling, when I was happy and when I was sad. When Jonathan smiled and cooed in return, I felt that he somehow understood and accepted me in spite of my faults; and I felt elated by this unique sharing. At times like these I knew that he was very much aware of my presence.

Walking is one of my favorite pastimes. Thus our meanderings together were a way for me to share with Jonathan something that also gave me great pleasure. I'm sure that he also looked forward to our outings, for whenever my wife said, "Do you want to take a walk with Daddy?" he flopped his hands and his eyes lit up in a smile, letting both of us know with what eagerness he greeted these little expeditions.

I felt proud when passersby complimented me on what a beautiful baby Jonathan was. He had a way about him. His big, beaming smile, his sparkling, intensely brown eyes and full head of jet-black hair seemed to draw people to him. His alertness and responsive interaction with them always resulted in his making immediate friends. He was irresistible!

As we wandered along, I frequently sang to him, and he in turn cooed back to me in time to the music. "Twinkle, Twinkle, Little Star" was a melody I had used to calm him and allay his cries since he was only one week old. He had heard it so often that it had become "his song," and as a result he seemed to derive much satisfaction from it, despite my off-key voice. He never grew tired of hearing it; and when there was a momentary lapse in the strain, he would urge me on with a cry, indicating his dissatisfaction at the pause.

When I carried Jonathan in the baby sling he would lay his head against my chest and place his fingers in my outstretched hand as he went to sleep. The touch of his soft face against my own body enhanced the sense of closeness I felt toward him. I guess it was really a love relationship from the start, a love that deepened and grew during these special times together. When he was older, Jonathan would jabber away at me as I carried him on my back until, calmed by the alternating motion of our jaunt together, his speech slackened and he ever so slowly laid his head against the nape of my neck and dropped off to sleep.

In the hushed still of the forest where we walked, the regular resonance of his breathing resembled a drum beating in time to the sounds of life around us. The rustling of leaves, stirred by an occasional puff of wind; the song of a robin overhead; and the distant murmur of a brook as it wound its way over impeding rocks coalesced to form an all-embracing presence. Everything enveloping us reflected the rhythm of my walk with Jonathan, and I felt in tune with him and with the beauty of nature about us. It was on these occasions that I felt an unusual sense of peace and tranquillity. I experienced an overwhelming love for my newborn son, and I felt that we were linked by a bond that was strong enough to transcend the ages. It was as if our companionship had entered into another plane, and there was now a union of our spirits.

At this point I would feel rejuvenated. I had become exquisitely sensitive to the world around us—to the natural ambience—to colors, smells, sights, and sounds. Although I might have taken that path many times in the past, my sensations now revealed things that I never knew existed.

Sometimes as I talked to Jonathan it seemed that I was really talking to myself, and I would feel in touch with my own center. His presence helped me to break out of my adult world in which everything was ordered and set, and allowed me to experience the world of childhood, where everything is free and spontaneous. Past memories, long since forgotten, of earlier years and relationships with my own family would surface, effortlessly, to my awareness. It was as if Jonathan was the door, the entryway, to my experiencing a new and different aspect of myself. At the same time, I felt even more intimately connected to him.

One of our walks particularly stands out in my mind. Jonathan had just fallen asleep on my back when the peaceful calm was broken by a strange occurrence: A loud, piercing, low-pitched cry, a cross between a seal barking and a donkey braying, resounded through the forest. Startled, I thought my senses were deceiving me. But a few minutes later I heard, once again, that peculiar note with its strange haunting quality. I had never heard anything like it. My first impulse was to run—from what I didn't know. But my curiosity overrode my fear. With Jonathan slumbering peacefully on my back, I stealthily moved in the direction of that unusual noise until, without warning, I came upon a large deer. Seemingly unafraid, it stood quietly gazing at us, as if wondering to itself, "What is this strange animal before me?" Then, after what seemed an interminable period, it slowly turned and strode off into the safety of the underbrush.

The mysterious quality of that experience amplified and heightened ever further the inspirational feeling that permeated our walks together. It was as if through Jonathan I was reaching into the world of wonder and enchantment. And there was no way of telling what awaited us there.

Feeling enthralled by and even reverent of these events, I had the urge to share my experiences with others. I began taking my tape recorder on our walks. And as Jonathan drifted off to sleep, I would talk into the microphone while walking through the forest. I imagined myself seated on the floor of a wooden cabin somewhere in the wilderness, speaking with a small and friendly group of fathers, as the embers in the fireplace brightly flickered, casting its intimate glow upon us.

I wanted to share not only the joy and beauty of this first experience of parenthood, but also the trials and trauma of it. Like fathers everywhere, I too was coping with the day-to-day efforts of working to earn a living to support my family while attempting to weather the vast changes in my life wrought by the birth of my first child. I wanted to tell other fathers that being able to experience a feeling of closeness with their newborn child makes the struggle more tolerable, even joyous. And it is this struggle along the road toward developing an intense and intimate companionship with my newborn son that I would like to share with you—and invite you to set out on your own journey with your own child.

·2·

The Birth

For me, everything began with the birth of Jonathan, so it is important that I start my account several weeks prior to this event. We continued to go out during the last several weeks before Claudia's delivery, perhaps as much or more so than we had previously. There was something exciting in enjoying ourselves fully up to the last minute. We knew that we were fully prepared now. We had gone to the childbirth education classes together, where we learned about the different levels of breathing that could be utilized to cope with labor pains. We had spent many hours together practicing, and now I felt a sense of pride and purpose in my coaching role. I had read several books in the last few months that dealt with exercises and general notions of labor and delivery.

Claudia had packed all of the necessary items in a bag, and we were ready to go at any time. We knew we had done all that was humanly possible in the way of preparation. I felt more relaxed during the days just before the delivery than I had during any time of the pregnancy. I felt very close to my wife, and I enjoyed the feeling of togetherness that we had.

It had been extremely hot, and as a result Claudia and I had been swimming in the ocean almost every weekend prior to her delivery. As I gazed at her protuberant abdomen, I felt both proud and protective of my wife. She had a sparkle to her eyes, a beaming smile, and her body was tanned and healthy looking. She seemed totally in harmony with the universe, and as I let my fantasies wander she became a great "earth mother" for me.

More than ever before, I now felt ready for that which lay ahead yet secretly hoped that Claudia would be late. Although I felt prepared, I was eager for any additional day that passed before the birth, and I enjoyed and savored them as if they were beautiful gifts of life. I was attempting to experience those days totally, drink them in, knowing that soon my life would change. A part of me would be receding into the background, symbolically dying, as another aspect—the father—emerged and was born.

The momentous day began on Tuesday, June 11, 1974. At about 12:30 A.M. Claudia said to me, "Hon, I'm having a lot of gas pains." I remember thinking, "Oh my God, you can't go into labor now. I need more time. I hope it's just indigestion." With that idea embedded in my mind I dropped back to sleep.

Claudia woke me at about 6:00 A.M. to say, "Hon, I've been awake since two in the morning. I've been having pains for the past four hours. I keep falling asleep in between, but they keep waking me up. I didn't want to wake you until I thought for sure they were real. I think I might be in labor."

At 8:00 Claudia went to the bathroom and passed a slightly blood-tinged mucous plug. I had gotten out my old obstetrics textbook and noted that the passage of the mucous plug indicated that the delivery was imminent and would occur within the next twenty-four hours. No question about it, this was going to be the day. At this point we called Claudia's doctor, who urged us to come in.

Within twenty minutes we were in his office. He examined Claudia and then, after she got dressed, asked me to join her in the room. "Well, congratulations," he said to the two of us. "You're going to have a baby soon." Then he nodded to Claudia and said, "You're in early labor. The baby's head is engaged; your cervix is two centimeters dilated and you're one hundred percent effaced. I'll call over now and tell the hospital you're on your way." I liked the way the doctor had included me, and the positive note of congratulations with which he had shared his findings with both of us.

We walked across the street to the hospital. There a volunteer, after asking Claudia to sit in a wheelchair, pushed her in the direction of the labor and delivery suite. Meanwhile, at the business office I made certain that all of the financial details were taken care of before I joined Claudia.

Claudia greeted me with a big smile and a hug. As I glanced around the room I saw a baby stethoscope on the other bed. It seemed almost to beckon to me, and I eagerly responded by placing the fetoscope over my head in an attempt to pick up any sounds I could from this large form within my wife's abdomen. But before I could listen further one of the nurses interrupted me by saying, "Yes, you may use the stethoscope." I said, "Oh, thank you, I appreciate that." I gathered that this was her way of asserting her authority and that I was supposed to ask before I used the stethoscope. However, her comment and the tone of her voice also had the effect of diminishing my enthusiasm, and I put the fetoscope down.

During the first few hours in the hospital, Claudia's labor continued to be fairly mild, and she experienced no great discomfort. We felt so relaxed that we might have been away on vacation. However, the starkness of the room continued to remind us that we were in a hospital and there was serious business ahead. I guess you almost expect a hospital to be bleak, and this one certainly didn't fail along those lines. The room was a sterile white, and there were no pictures on the walls. The furniture consisted of two beds, Claudia's and an empty one to the right, a stand beside each, and two chairs. The room also contained a bathroom, which served to make it a self-contained chamber.

Even at this late hour we were still unable to select a name; it was a toss-up between Alicia and Rena. We never even bothered to discuss boys' names because we were both convinced that we were going to have a girl. Also, over six weeks ago we had decided that if we had a boy we would name him Jonathan David. The name had a nice ring to it, and we liked it. Moreover, it was close to Jacob, my grandfather's name.

As the labor slowly progressed, I tried to ease the passage of time by telling Claudia stories. My saga was interrupted by the doctor's arrival at 12:30 P.M. He examined her and then announced, "Well, you're about four centimeters dilated. You're moving along slowly. We're going to help things along a bit and break your water bag." With those words he took out a long stylet, probed around with it, then punctured Claudia's membranes, which resulted in a sudden flow of liquid all over her legs. He then plugged her up to a machine.

Let me tell you what I mean by that. He reached up into the birth canal and placed electrodes on the baby's head. He explained that the monitoring equipment would provide a continuous check on how the baby was doing during labor. If the heartbeat slowed, indicating that the baby was in distress, they would know it and emergency measures (such as a rapid cesarean section) could be taken.

Suddenly everything changed. Whereas before we had felt relaxed and at ease, joking and rather carefree, the labor was now a very serious business. Claudia's contractions became more intense almost immediately, and she needed to pant to cope with them. She was no longer interested in hearing stories.

It seemed as if the machine had taken over. In fact, it was now physically located where I had been sitting. Initially I felt reluctant to touch it. After all, the doctor had placed it where he wanted it to be, right? The fact that it took my place was irrelevant. Maybe it was supposed to take my place. But the machine could not hold my wife's hand, or wipe her brow or whisper words of encouragement and support. That was something only I could do.

The situation was rapidly deteriorating. My chair was directly behind this technological marvel, which meant that to hold Claudia's hand I had to reach over the machine, subjecting my whole body to the most ridiculous of contortions and straining my neck and back. After about twenty minutes of trying to do this I thought, "I have to do something before I become a casualty of labor." I got up and looked around for Claudia's doctor or one of the nurses. But, mysteriously, nobody was around.

So what do you do when a machine has taken your place? Do you kick it, curse it, throw it out the window? Obviously I couldn't do any of those things. (I did, of course, give it hell.) The machine was there to stay. After all, it was there for our benefit. "Fine, but why did it have to take my seat?" I asked myself. Finally I decided to take matters into my own hands. I tried to find a place for my chair on the opposite side of the bed, but that wouldn't work because the bed was wedged smack against the wall. Then I tried to move both the bed and the machine to the right. Fantastic! That was the solution. I was now able to find a small place for my chair on the left side of the bed. I was still somewhat scrunched against the wall, but at least I could hold Claudia's hand and be close to her without developing a stiff neck or throwing my back out.

Once I had taken the initiative in moving the recording equipment, I began to notice the positive benefits. It made me aware of how intense Claudia's contractions were, when they were starting, and when they began to tail off in intensity. Thus it enhanced my efforts to effectively coach her through the labor.

Claudia was now laboring with much greater effort and experiencing some pain intermittently. The minutes were slowly ticking away.

It was now 1:30 in the afternoon. Only infrequently did hospital staff enter our little sanctuary. We were essentially alone. It seemed as if Claudia and I had been deserted to struggle on by ourselves with the relentless forces that pushed her ever forward and closer to delivery.

I would attempt to coach Claudia by watching the progress of the contractions on the monitor, encouraging her to pant as she had been taught to do in her childbirth education classes, and letting her know when the contractions had reached their peak. I felt like a coxswain and sweated profusely as I shouted my words of support and encouragement: "OK, Claudia, it's getting stronger, it's getting stronger, you're doing fine. OK, now it's reached its peak, just a little more. OK, it's going down, it's getting weaker. OK, it's almost down. There, it's down."

Claudia and I worked together as a team—she, of course, doing all the physical work. I, for my part, would wipe her perspiring brow with a washcloth, alternately wetting it with a little bit of water and putting it into her mouth to relieve her thirst. As the labor progressed, I experienced a powerful sense of intimacy with my wife. I felt involved, an integral part of the whole process.

I tried to be physically close to Claudia throughout the labor. I think my continued presence annoyed the nursing staff. I was infringing on their territory, and there was little for them to do. They suggested that I leave and get a bite to eat, but that wasn't necessary as I had brought my lunch with me. I think this irritated them even more. That bleak little labor room became my whole world. If I needed to empty my bladder, I used the toilet in the room. If I got hungry, I grabbed a sandwich or took a bite out of the apple that I had brought along. I never left Claudia's side, and I resisted all efforts to lure me away. My continual presence, I felt, was important to her, for I sensed that she needed my support and encouragement. But beyond that, I wanted and needed to be a part of these events, to be involved and a participant in this powerful process that was unfolding.

I enjoyed coaching Claudia; in a way I found it to be fun. Claudia, too, in little ways, let me know how important my presence was to her, and this was something that made me feel proud. I also felt as if I was Claudia's protector, there to intercede between her and the real world. I now saw her as weak and exposed, unable to shield herself from the events that were unfolding around her. As long as I remained there, I would be able to keep her under my protective wing. If I left, there was no telling what might happen.

As the afternoon rolled by, the labor continued to progress. Then the contractions began to change. The needle on the monitoring equipment began to leap about the page, seeming to move to a higher peak with each passing wave. The contractions were so intense now that Claudia had to pant and blow, the highest level of breathing she had been taught. We were getting close. Claudia was now clearly in transition. She was beginning to feel very tired and somewhat frightened, because in spite of her breathing the contractions were very intense. She appealed to me: "Marty, I don't know if I can take it. The pain is just unbearable. I feel like I may need to have something."

"Just hold on a little bit longer," I said as I wiped her brow. "You're almost there, you're doing fine, honey. You're doing fine."

A short time later the doctor came in to examine her. He told her encouragingly, "You're doing fine. You're close to being completely dilated and are almost to the point where you can push. You're going to have a nice baby." I was shocked to see a nurse in the back of the room shake her head and say to the doctor, loud enough for both my wife and me to hear, "She's not going to push that baby out." The doctor himself was taken aback. But he recovered quickly, grabbed the nurse, and threw his arm around her as if he was going to dance around the room with her and said with a big laugh, "Ho, ho. We all kind of kid around with each other and sort of disagree at times. Don't mind us. We're all just one big happy team. She's really a great nurse." But the damage had already been done. I couldn't believe she'd said that. She had showed a total lack of understanding and awareness of our needs. I was appalled by her insensitivity. I was beginning to feel lost in a sea of negativism in which there was no support whatsoever. Of course, we did have our doctor, who in some ways was a kind of positive life raft. He was encouraging, and he did at least make a fumbling effort to apologize for the nurse's behavior. Nevertheless, he seemed unable to protect Claudia from the destructive comments of the nursing staff. As a result, I felt a growing need to form a protective cocoon around her to shield her from these negative onslaughts.

In addition, because I was so involved in the process of labor, I felt that in belittling Claudia's efforts the nurse had also belittled me. Frankly, I was furious. And this sense of anger and aloneness enhanced my own feelings of anxiety. But I knew I had to keep the anger in check if I didn't want to be distracted from our overriding goal of producing a normal baby.

All during this period Claudia had felt the urge to push but continued to hold the impulse in check. Finally, after what seemed like ages, her doctor said, "Now it's okay to push. Go ahead, push now, push." With these words I felt that we were at last hurtling down the gun lap of a long race. This was it; the checkered flag was raised.

It was now about 3:45 in the afternoon. Claudia began to push in earnest and became almost purple in the face with the effort. I tried to encourage her, but this was really her struggle. Each time she had a contraction I raised her up, and she would push very hard for a minute. Then I allowed her to stop, lie back, and take a few deep breaths before we started the cycle all over again. This was the technique we had learned in our childbirth education class, and it seemed to work. After ten minutes of this the doctor indicated that she was ready to go into the delivery room.

Before I could join Claudia, I had to change into a scrub suit. The thought that she might give birth without my being present increased the speed and enthusiasm with which I changed. The scrub suit seemed to have been made for someone six inches taller and fifty pounds heavier. I pulled the cord at my waist as tight as I could, took a deep breath, prayed that my pants wouldn't fall down, and marched into the delivery room.

Attired in scrub suit, cap, and mask I took my place at the foot of the delivery-room table. Not bothering to use the high chair that was available I stood there talking to Claudia and wiping her brow in between contractions. Whenever she had a contraction I would elevate her back as I had done before, urging: "Push, Claudia, push, push. You're doing fine. Push, push." Then I would allow her to come back down for a few breaths and lift her up again. After about ten minutes of this Claudia was becoming very tired. She had been pushing like mad and expending an incredible amount of energy. Moreover, the contractions were very intense now. My scrub suit was dripping with sweat, and I felt an incredible amount of pressure and tension. It felt as if we were *both* working very hard.

"Now hold it," the doctor said, and Claudia began to take short, panting breaths. "Look, Claudia," I said suddenly excited. "You can see hair!" But she was concentrating on her contractions too much to be able to see anything else and didn't take as much as a glance at the mirror that was suspended below the bright surgical lights overhead.

As Claudia began to push with the next contraction, a full head of dark, black hair became more visible. "Look at all the hair, Claudia!" At this point the doctor reached for the scissors. "My God," I thought, "those scissors are huge. Is he going to use those on my wife?" This was immediately followed by another thought, "My God, that's an enormous episiotomy." He snipped once, twice. "That's enough," I wanted to shout as he snipped a third time. Then I thought, "Oh, my God, he's doing it again," as he snipped even a fourth, fifth, and sixth time. I winced in pain as if I myself had been slashed and turned to Claudia, who seemed not to have noticed that the doctor was cutting away at her vital parts. "That bastard," I thought. "Why did he have to cut her like that?"

Claudia had now been in the delivery room for close to twenty minutes, and still she was pushing very hard. Finally I heard those words I dreaded: "We're going to have to put on forceps," said the doctor. Claudia said nothing. She couldn't have talked even if she'd wanted to. For her, the only reality was the contraction of each moment, which must have seemed an eternity. I felt disappointed. We were almost there—just a little more time, a little more effort, and we would be "there." "Oh," I said, "couldn't she possibly push the baby out with a couple more pushes?" "No," he replied. "She's really been in labor too long; I'm going to have to help her along. I'm going to have to put on forceps." The doctor was right, I realized. Claudia had already been in labor for almost fourteen hours, and she was growing increasingly more fatigued. I felt a sadness that we had to rely on forceps, and at the same time I was concerned that the forceps might harm the baby. We had come such a long way together, and now we were so close, so near. . . . I didn't finish my thought because the doctor had put the forceps in place. But before he could touch them further, Claudia, sensing it was now or never, made one final effort and it was enough.

I heard a loud cry even before the baby was completely delivered, and the next thing I knew there was this beautiful baby boy before my eyes. I couldn't believe it, and for a brief instant I felt stunned by his size. When I saw him, I began to laugh. I laughed and laughed almost uncontrollably, as if some unseen floodgates had suddenly been released. It was a laugh of joy and happiness, and I hugged my wife and kept kissing her as I repeated, "Look! Look! Look at the baby, Claudia, look! We have a baby, we have a baby boy. We produced a boy!"

Claudia, for her part, was still somewhat exhausted and in a state of shock, not yet completely comprehending the situation. I don't mean shock in the sense of her blood pressure dropping, but rather, in the sense of a suspension of all her thoughts. She replied rather weakly, but with a smile, "Oh, a boy, oh, fantastic!"

He looked absolutely incredible from the moment I saw him. His wide open, searching eyes seemed to take in everything, giving him an air of alertness from the very beginning. He had striking features, a beautiful full head of hair, and he already looked much older and more mature than other newborn babies I had seen. I felt very close to him almost immediately, as if he had always been a part of our family and our life. Accompanying this feeling was a sense of intense closeness to Claudia that seemed mediated by his presence. I was absolutely bowled over and surprised at my reaction. I thought I wanted a girl, but from my reaction you would have thought that I had been anticipating a boy all along.

I was absolutely swept off my feet and carried away by the power of this moment. I was beside myself: I wanted to hop, skip, and jump. I felt like shouting, singing, and dancing; but instead I laughed so hard that I cried. I was completely flooded with emotion. Seeing my son being born, seeing him for the first time, was the most incredible experience I can recall ever having. I felt high. I was reeling from the power of the birth. I felt that we had finally arrived.

·3·

Engrossment: The Newborn's Impact

My experience of my son s birth was intensely personal, just as yours will be with your child.[1] I have tried to communicate it in a way that will draw your feelings into it and give you the full taste and flavor of the experience. In other words, I have been sharing my son's birth with you as if we were sitting together in that warm and friendly mountain cabin of my imagination. Now I want to begin talking about what *your* experience may be with your own child. I hope that you too will have an opportunity to experience a sense of joy, fascination, and well-being in relation to your newborn. I call this feeling *engrossment.* Helping you to become engrossed with your baby is the principal goal of this book.

Bonding and attachment are general terms describing the link, the connection, between parent and child. Most of the work in this area has focused on the mother's early bond with her baby. *Engrossment* is a term that I coined to specifically describe the link or bond of the father to his newborn. Clearly, however, engrossment has many similiarities to the bonding process that occurs with mothers and babies.

Many fathers throughout the world pay little attention to their infant children from the time of birth; or perhaps present at the birth, they subsequently drop out of their children's lives, setting in their mind a magical deadline two to three years hence, of when to become more involved with their children, of when to have a relationship. These men don't know what they are missing! For the father's experience of engrossment in his newborn is a unique gift for the father. And it is he who will benefit perhaps as much or more than his child.

The word *engrossment* refers to a father's sense of absorption, preoccupation, and interest in his baby. He feels gripped and held by this feeling. He has an intense desire to look at his baby, to touch and hold him. It is as if he is hooked, drawn to his newborn child by some involuntary force over which he has no control. He doesn't will it to happen, it just does. Often he has this experience when he sees his baby for the first time, and especially if he participates in the birth of his child.

I first studied new fathers' involvement with their babies while I was completing my psychiatric training in London in 1971. Working with first-time fathers, I explored their feelings about their newborns. It was from this study that the concept of engrossment developed. Engrossment, or father bonding, as it has also been called, has since been the object of a great deal of study both in America and other countries. Engrossment appears to be a universal process, an innate potential in *all* fathers.

But engrossment means more than involvement. The term *engross,* from which it is derived, means to "make large." When a father feels engrossed in his baby, the infant has become larger than life for him. Not only that, but fathers suddenly feel as if they themselves have grown. They feel bigger, stronger, older, more powerful. With his engrossment in his baby, a father feels an increased sense of self-esteem and worth, a validation of his existence, of his role as a parent and a father.

Your own feelings of love and engrossment may or may not surface at the first sight of your child. They sometimes take awhile to develop. But when they do emerge, you will experience a sense of exhilaration and harmony. And although the intensity of your emotions fades away over the first few weeks, you will find that the feelings do return later, perhaps in a mellower, more mature way, as a foundation for your continuing loving involvement with your child.

The initial, peak feelings of engrossment actually consist of seven different experiences. I will describe them partly in the words of some of the first-time fathers I worked with in London.

1.–*There is an intense visual awareness of the baby.* The father delights in looking at his own baby as opposed to other babies. He perceives his newborn as attractive, pretty, and beautiful.

One English father said:

> "I couldn't get over it. I suppose what it was, in the afternoon, I walked up and down and looked in that room up there and they all looked a bit ugly, a bit rubbery, and then when she came out she looked so beautiful, really, a little gem, so beautiful."

The newborn's face itself also has a powerful impact on the father. It is not only seen as beautiful but also makes the father aware of the baby as an individual. For example, a father who did not witness his child's birth stated:

> "There was much more character in the child's face than I ever thought there would be at that stage. I mean, it didn't remind me of anybody, but it seemed to have a personality immediately. . . . It was absolutely incredible, the sight itself."

2.–*There is an intense tactile awareness of the baby.* Fathers want to touch their baby, to have physical contact with him. They want to pick the baby up, to hold him and play with him. One father expressed his extreme pleasure in his baby this way:

> "I feel great, just great; can't stop picking her up—really a strong feeling of pleasure. She wriggles in your hands; she wriggles when she's against your chest and in your arms."

The father is impressed by the soft feeling of the baby's skin, by how smooth it is. When I asked one father how it felt to touch his baby, he replied:

> "Oh, incredibly soft; one hears the expression as soft as a baby's backside, I suppose, but then, on the other hand, when I touched it, it seemed incredibly soft, like velvet."

3.–*The baby appears distinctly different from other babies.* The father is very aware of the unique features of his baby. He can describe him in elaborate detail and may feel he could even recognize him in a crowd. He is also more likely to emphasize the baby's resemblance to himself rather than to his wife.

One father described his feelings for his newborn in this way: "It's a marvelous feeling, especially as he looks like me." When asked how the baby looked like him, he said:

> "He's got a longish body already, although he's very light in weight. He's got large hands like me, he's got long feet, he's got large ears, he's got a broad nose like me, he's got a little chin with a cleft I think. He's got my wife's hair, long silky black hair, and her eyes—at the moment—which are brown. I definitely would be able to recognize him by his face, and if I wasn't sure about the face, I could definitely go by the hands and feet. I think I could pick him out of a crowd."

4.–*The baby looks perfect, just right.* Despite some of the baby's awkwardness and unsightly aspects, the father sees him as the epitome of perfection. This is captured in the words of another English father:

> "The little nervous system seems to be in its first stages. It seems not to be completely coordinated yet. . . . The legs seem to be shaking about as if they're a bit uncoordinated. But it all seems just right. It seems as though all these little systems are going into action—the eyes, the ears, the neck, the nervous system. Everything seems to be going into action and everything seems to be *just right, just right.*"

5.–*The father feels a strong attraction to the infant and focuses his attention on him.* Another father said:

> "When I come up to see me wife, and I say, "Hi! How's things, everything all right, you need anything?" And then I go look at the kid and then I pick her up and then I put her down and then I say, 'Hi! Is everything all right?' And then I go back to the kid. I keep going back to the kid. It's like a magnet. That's what I can't get over, the fact that I feel like that."

This focusing on the baby can make him seem larger: One father said:

> "Hey, she looked a bit bigger that night than she does tonight. I suppose, the birth, things are perhaps exaggerated or magnified a bit."

6.–*The father feels elated and exhilarated.* He may even describe himself as high, a feeling usually experienced whether he was present at the birth or not. He feels stunned, stoned, dazed, off the ground, ten feet tall, taken away, taken out of himself. For example, a father who was present at his child's birth said:

> "I took a look at it and I took a look at the face and I left the ground—just left the ground! I thought, 'Oh! Jesus Christ! This is marvelous.' "

7.–*The father feels an increased sense of self-esteem.* He feels proud, bigger, more mature, and older. A twenty-three-year-old father said:

> "I just feel a bit older now. I'm a father, a father at last. I feel I've got something of me own. I look at it and I say, 'I done that—I done that, it's mine.' "

The father is likely to be surprised at the powerful impact the infant has on him and at the extent of all his feelings. His previous attitudes and expectations about the baby may even change. A father who wanted a boy but got a girl instead said:

> "I thought if it was going to be a boy and everything was going to be great, we could go out and jump around together and play about together. I was thinking about eighteen months, two years, two and a half years, then we'd start to have a relationship. And I thought for the first eighteen months it would be for the wife and everything would be fine for her and I'd just take it easy. But it wasn't like that at all. It was completely different. The kid was born—and I was there—and I really had a strong feeling toward her."

The baby's normal behavior, his normal reflexes, just the fact that he moves and looks about, all enhance the father's engrossment in his child. This is dramatically illustrated by a first-time father who stated:

> "I was so surprised to find that it was already, even at this age, doing certain things—like moving itself around. I thought it was going to be an object that would just be there. But it was looking around and gripping. At least I think it was gripping. You put your finger in its hand, and it was holding on . . . and when they just wrapped it up and put it in the cot by the side it immediately took on somebody—somebody that one could look at and touch; and it moved immediately. I felt suddenly I had a daughter! I didn't just have a baby."

These are the feelings that constitute engrossment. But if you don't feel intensely hooked up and involved with your own baby at first, don't berate yourself or give up. For some fathers the relationship evolves more gradually. T. Berry Brazelton is a renowned pediatrician who has done extensive work on parents and infants. When his own first child was born he was disappointed that he didn't feel as much emotion as he'd expected. Then, at about eight weeks, his baby began to smile at him and he felt himself responding, becoming engrossed. "I was caught as most young fathers are," he said. "From then on it was easy sailing as I became more and more involved with my baby."[2]

There are all kinds of situations that can interfere with a father's engrossment. For example, if he and his wife have had no childbirth education training she may perceive her labor contractions as much more painful than would otherwise be the case, and the labor and delivery may appear to be completely out of control. The father may feel unsure of exactly how he can help. His fear and anxiety, intensified by the chaos of the situation, can prevent him from feeling initially engrossed despite his presence at the birth.

If the wife's health is poor, if she was ill during the pregnancy, if there are complications during labor and delivery, or an emergency cesarean section is required that excludes the father from the delivery room, he may have a hard time focusing on the baby immediately. All of his energy may be taken up with his relief at his wife's being okay. Concern about her health and the frightening fear of losing her can combine to make it difficult to experience the newborn. Then too, if the baby is unresponsive or sedated at birth, perhaps because the mother has received excessive premedication, the father may have trouble feeling immediately close to his newborn because of its lack of activity.

Concerns about the newborn's health can alter the emergence of engrossment in the father, particularly if the baby is born prematurely or with serious birth anomalies. The parent mourns the loss of the hoped-for child, which can prevent him from bonding to the child who has actually been born.

In the delivery room itself there are many things going on that can potentially hinder the father's focus on the baby. There is the hustle and bustle of nurses, students, obstetricians, nursing aides, and anesthesiologists, all performing different tasks. In some hospitals various procedures are performed on the infant that take him away from both parents. For example, he may be placed in an isolette in the far corner of the room. If the mother has had an episiotomy (a small incision that serves to widen the birth canal), she may be distracted by her physician's ministrations. Following the birth the infant may be carried to the nursery, where mother and father may have no further contact with their newborn for the next twelve to twenty-four hours. Hospital procedures and the attitude of the hospital staff in general can either draw a parent to the infant or hinder engrossment.

Anything that causes the father fear or anxiety or otherwise pressures him, whether it be problems in the hospital, at home, or at work or school, can make him temporarily unavailable to experience the full impact of his baby. This is regrettable, but it can be overcome later. The best way for you as a father to become engrossed immediately is to be present at your child's birth, for this experience is a singular one in its impact and explosive power. It even has the capacity to break through any negative feelings you may have had about children.

Fathers who are present at the birth feel a sense of identity with their infants that is manifested time and again by the words, "When you see it born you know it's yours." One Scottish father put it like this:

> "The fact that you actually see it born—you *know* that it's yours. I'm not suggesting that if you don't go into the deliv-

ery room they swap them. But you can see your wife actually giving birth. And you know this is something the two of you have produced together."

The importance of becoming engrossed in your baby is paramount. Fathers who are not initially engrossed describe themselves as feeling distant, not much like fathers, and unconnected to their infants. One father I talked to felt as if he was on top of the ceiling, looking down at his wife and child at the time of the birth, an impartial observer. He was in tears as he described his later feelings of uninvolvement toward his infant. He felt that something was wrong with him, and he was angry and disturbed about his lack of excitement. After talking with this young father I looked through my notes about the birth and realized that his newborn did not begin breathing immediately, and he had been fearful for its welfare. To cope with this fear he had distanced himself, cut off his feelings, which prevented him from becoming engrossed in his child. With support, fathers in this situation can still experience engrossment.

The feeling of being distant from your newborn can be very painful, and the pain can be even more intense if you remember that your own father was uninvolved and unavailable to you as you were growing up. This is your chance, your opportunity to break that negative chain.

The key to hooking up with your baby is contact, physical contact. And it's important for you to really focus your attention on your baby when you hold him. Really be with him. If your thoughts are elsewhere, this will come between the two of you like a brick wall. Here is an example of the importance of contact in the emergence of engrossment. A twenty-four-year-old first-time father who was not present at his child's birth told me later:

"The nurse just sort of plopped him in my hands. I didn't feel much of anything. I didn't feel like a father. I didn't feel like he was mine."

But during the next few days he went to the hospital and saw his child frequently. He had an opportunity to look at him, touch him, and hold him. He then said:

> "I began to feel more and more like a father. I began to feel that he was mine. I didn't feel that way at first."

So don't be too hard on yourself if you don't immediately feel the full flush of excitement of the birth and the magnetic power of your new infant. Give yourself a chance. Allow yourself to experience the baby, to take him in. It is never too late. Allow all of your senses to be touched by your child, and you will be surprised at the way your feelings of closeness will grow.

Even though engrossment is a universal process and an innate potential among all fathers, it does not occur in a vacuum. It requires the crucial ingredient of contact with your little baby in order for its full force to explode upon the scene. In the pages ahead, I shall explain more about how this experience of engrossment can be both realized and reinforced.

•4•

Family Bonding: Together at Last

> "The delivery room was the end of something that had gone on for nine months, and the recovery room was the beginning of something else. And somewhere between the two, I think the boundary existed where the end of one thing and the beginning of something else happened; and our relationship started to develop in the recovery room."
>
> —Words of a father after the birth of his first child

That first wailing cry of your baby is an overwhelming experience. Your daughter is here! She has arrived after all this waiting! You feel a release of all kinds of emotion—joy, pride, excitement—and you may have a hard time containing this first surge of feelings. Hug your wife and tell her how proud you are of her and how close you feel. Sharing these feelings intensifies the closeness.

While some fathers immediately feel close to their wives and babies in the delivery room, others are distracted by the lack of privacy as well as the numerous activities occurring at that time. The sheer number of people creates a sense of chaos and bustle. There are usually several nurses in the room and often more than one doctor. If the delivery takes place in a university medical center, there are also medical and nursing students on hand, further adding to the confusion.

A young father told me about his experience:

> "The delivery room was real hectic—a lot of bustling and movement, and there were a lot of other people demanding

> attention. Not that they were really demanding my attention. But they were there and just by their presence they were a distraction."

Although you and your wife may hold the baby briefly following her birth, she is soon whisked away to have her reflexes and level of responsiveness checked as well as to have any mucus from her nostrils, mouth, and lungs sucked out. Usually they clean off the white, waxy substance (vernix) unless you specify otherwise, wipe off any coated blood, and then wrap her in a blanket before returning her to you and your wife. Then in a few minutes she is removed again to be measured and weighed. She may have silver nitrate or antibiotic ointment put into her eyes and be given a brief bath.

It is extremely frustrating to have the baby on the other side of the room in an isolette while all the delivery-room procedures are being carried out. You can tolerate this period better if you know that at the end of it you and your wife will have some uninterrupted time with your baby in the recovery room. If you don't have an opportunity to spend several unbroken hours together you will feel disappointed and empty, as though you've been cheated. You and your wife want to hold and cuddle that little baby, and it is absolutely imperative that you get to do that as soon as possible. Mothers and fathers have an urgent need for physical contact with their newborn infant. How soon that can happen will depend on the kind of birth facility you're in and the philosophy of both the hospital and the doctor.

The doctor usually delivers the placenta within the first fifteen minutes after the birth, so your wife must still remain on the delivery-room table. If she has had an episiotomy, she may have to stay there for an additional fifteen to thirty minutes.

Not only will you feel frustrated and distracted during this initial thirty to forty-five minutes after the birth, but you are likely to be disconcerted if you haven't experienced the high of engrossment with your baby. Just remember that fear, anxiety, uncertainty, and the confusion of the birth itself can interfere with your initial closeness to your baby. Your feelings for her will have a greater opportunity to blossom when you are alone with her, when you are not buffeted by people and demands.

During the first moments after the birth while mother and child are being cared for, your wife will desperately want to know what is happening and will appreciate your describing the scene to her. You can give her a running account, as I did with Claudia: "Look at him—he has big, searching eyes and he's looking around the room He's huge. He's got really long arms and long legs, and everything looks just perfect. He's beautiful!"

While they're working on the baby you can attempt to capture her on film. This isn't as good as holding her, but at least you'll be doing something to enhance your memory of your child at birth, something that will give you and your wife much pleasure later on. One new father put it this way:

> "I wanted to grab her, but they were taking care of her. I wanted to hold her and touch her and see what she was like. I couldn't do that at that point. So what I did was I grabbed her on film. I was real intent on getting as many pictures as I could while she was out of my hands."

The longer she is out of your hands, the more frustrating it becomes. You want to get ahold of that little bundle of energy. And you want to share your feelings in privacy with your wife as soon as possible. One new father commented on these feelings and the barriers he felt in the delivery room:

> "I was fascinated and curious about my baby, and I wanted to touch her and get to know her. But I really couldn't do it, I couldn't do all those things. There were all those constraints on us in the delivery room. I had to wear the mask, and I was wearing all kinds of garbage on my body and I just couldn't get to know her. Plus there were all these other people. So I didn't feel like a relationship with her really coalesced until I got into the recovery room. The recovery room was time for us to really get to know her."

It is in the recovery room that you and your wife can finally be alone with your baby for the first time. Here you can cuddle and explore your child. Here you can cry and laugh together without any concern about being seen by the world at large. This is a time when all the surging energy activated during the labor and delivery can be expressed. Many parents release sobs of joy. The nine months of anticipation and waiting, as well as the frustration, anxiety, and fears, finally burst forth in a flood of relief. And merged with this is a powerful feeling of exhilaration. All has gone well, and the baby is here!

Despite these high emotions, there is a sense of tranquillity in the recovery room. One father told me that being there, protected and undisturbed, was like entering a peaceful lagoon following a raging hurricane (the birth). This time together is a transcendent, almost reverent, once-in-a-lifetime experience during which you suddenly feel in touch with yourself, your wife, and your child. You have a new closeness, an unusual sensitivity and awareness.

This feeling is captured in the words of a young father:

> "We certainly felt closer. I can't speak for my wife, but I certainly felt this closeness between us. I also felt an awful lot of vibrations toward the child. He was playing a part in this. There was a three-way play at this stage—something was making us feel even closer than we had before."

It is in this tranquil, protected setting that family bonding frequently begins to blossom, when you and your wife and child begin to come together as a family. For this reason, many parents refer to the recovery room as the bonding room. In alternate birth centers and home deliveries, it is the room where the delivery itself has occurred. Essentially, it can be anywhere, as long as it is a place where your new family can be free of disturbances. Although the setting may be a simple one, what takes place there is not so simple.

A new mother described the newness and elation of this moment:

> "I found that I was really concentrating on the baby as well as on us as a new family. It was another new face in our life. That new beginning is that we are no longer just my husband and I. We are a little family now, and it was really a kind of fun time. Oh, we're a family! Here we are, and it's the first time, and here we are together!"

Hospital staff may intermittently enter the room to take your wife's pulse and blood pressure. If these people are sensitive and caring, you will probably not even notice them and will not experience their brief presence as an interruption. However, during this period you are in a highly vulnerable state in which your euphoria can easily be destroyed by insensitive comments or by frequent disturbances and disruptions. Fortunately, those staff members who have been a part of the labor and delivery process are frequently also touched by the unique forces of the birth and are responsive and sensitive to the new parents. You experience this sensitivity of the staff almost intuitively, and it becomes an important part of your adjustment following the birth. You begin to realize that people around you understand and really do care. And this is essential.

As a doctor, when I see a couple with their newborn at such a moment I feel a need to tiptoe about, for I instinctively know that something very significant is taking place. It's as if you've ventured into a place of worship, into another age where time stands still and the experience of the moment seems to go on forever. The parents talk in hushed tones, giggling quietly and smiling, talking to their baby, exploring their baby together. There is a sense of blissful excitement on their faces.

As you gaze at your tiny infant, you may experience an overwhelming urge to protect her. One father said:

> "Just this little teeny, weak, helpless person that was mine! What goes through your mind is she's disoriented and scared. She needs me to protect her and take care of her and orient her to the world and help her make sense of it, to buffer her experience in some way. I wasn't protecting her from anything out there, really. Nothing dangerous is going to happen. It was more like wanting to enfold her and warm her and comfort her and caress her and soften the harshness of the birth experience."

Perhaps when you are finally alone with your wife and child you will begin to call the new baby by her name. Earlier, in the delivery room, the baby was still a he, she, or it. It is the enhanced intimacy of the bonding room that allows you to start calling your baby by the name you have debated on for months and probably rehearsed over and over again with your wife until the sound of it seemed just right. Uttering it for the first time is akin to a naming ceremony. When I felt reunited with my own wife and little baby in the recovery room, I pushed the baby's blanket back, gazed at his big brown eyes and said with a sigh of relief, "Well, Claudia, we've got a baby, we've got a Jonathan David." And from then on we always called him Jonathan. Calling your little baby by her name actually enhances your engrossment in her. Repeating her name as you talk to her is an outpouring of your energy and involvement that draws you even closer to her.

You will find it fascinating to watch your wife with your newborn, cooing softly to her, absorbed in her. You may feel a special tenderness and love for your wife at this moment. Now she is no longer only your wife, your sweetheart, your lover, but also a mother, the mother of your child, the mother of the child who is a part of both of you. Perhaps she has always been your friend and confidante, but having gone through this trial by fire together deepens the levels of all these relationships.

It may seem to you that your wife has been a mother all of her life, so loving and tender she is with the baby. On one level it seems so easy, so automatic, so natural; yet on another level it is absolutely incredible, beyond belief. For nine months your baby has been slowly growing in your wife's womb. It's been frustrating for you because your wife has been describing what the baby feels like inside her—how she moves, kicks, hiccups—and you could only try to feel it from the outside. Now your lovable little baby is really here, in your arms.

Your voices almost seem to echo in that tiny room after all the action and chaos of the delivery room. But that seems like a faraway world. Now you are left alone to hook up, to "become a family." Some fathers get into bed with their wives so they can cradle her and their newborn together. This would be perfectly natural at home, but you may feel inhibited about doing it at the hospital. You can hug your wife as she lies there with your infant in her arms, and feel close and related to both of them. Tell your wife again how well she did, and how proud you are of her. She may be too exhausted to respond verbally, but she will appreciate everything you say. Even years later, she will remember the feelings that your loving words triggered.

This time together is very significant in your relationship with your wife. Many women speak of how meaningful it was for them to have their men present during the labor, delivery, and immediately after the birth. They feel a heightened intimacy with their husbands, a new dimension in their marriages.

As you hug your wife and baby you may feel a pang of sadness mixed with joy as you realize that as much as you want to hold on to this moment, you cannot stop the clock. The image of your infant suddenly all grown up may flash before you, and you may wonder if you will be able to protect her from the struggles that lie ahead. You want to make time stand still so that the pleasure of this moment can go on, unending, so you will never have to face your child's growing apart from you.

The attempt to stay close to our children continues even as we learn to accept their increasing independence. And this begins, or at least the illusion of it begins, right from birth.

This struggle is vividly captured by a first-time father describing his experience with his newborn in the recovery room:

> "I was looking at her, looking at her hands and looking at her feet and listening to her, trying to capture her in some way and hold her. I wasn't holding her physically, I don't mean in that way. But I felt a real strong need to hold her somehow inside, in my head. That's why we were crying for the first week. It was like the harder we tried to hold on to her, she changed instantly from what she was into what she is. Every moment, she was changing into something else—a different kind of person. And it was like we were losing her all the time. It was like we never had a chance to know her as a newborn. I mean as a real brand-new newborn, because already she was responding and changing and doing things and crying differently. These incredible changes were taking place and there was no way we could hang on to that moment, that beginning."

But even this longing to stop the clock cannot diminish the thrill of seeing and touching your little baby for the first time. You may initially find yourself in a state of shock, still having a hard time comprehending everything that's happened. If so, try to share your feelings with your wife. If you hang back and say nothing, she may get the feeling that you don't care, and that would be a devastating beginning. Try to tell her how overwhelmed you feel. This will not only be important for her but for you as well, because the act of sharing will help you to break out of your dazed state.

The bonding room is also a unique opportunity to share your uncertainties and fears, some of which you may have kept from your wife during the final months of the pregnancy. Perhaps you were afraid to verbalize your feelings because of superstitious fears—"If I talk about it, it might happen." Now you don't have to hold your feelings back; you can let them go.

You'll also appreciate hearing your wife's praise of your own efforts. Perhaps when the doctor or nurses were not as responsive or caring as you would have wanted, you gave your wife all the emotional support you could. You probably racked your brains trying to say the right thing, to encourage and help. And if your wife was doing well during labor and had a helpful doctor and nurse, you may have wondered if your presence made any difference at all. It is not only your wife who needs support during this time, you also need it. Seeing her in labor and perhaps fearful and in pain may have increased your own fears and feelings of vulnerability. Now you need to have her tell you how much you've helped.

This time belongs to your family, to use in the way that is the most meaningful for you. Some parents bring their favorite music into the room to enhance the atmosphere of this special time. One father told me of composing a song on his guitar in the bonding room, pouring all his feelings for his child into the song, a kind of special love song between father and baby. You and your wife might also enjoy singing to your baby, changing the words of familiar songs so that they're specifically directed to her. You might tape record the sounds she makes and take pictures of her.

The closeness you now feel with your infant is an important first experience that will make you want to stay close. It will encourage you to continue to have intimate contact with your child in the days, months, and years ahead. It is another positive reinforcing experience. And it will be a memory that you will always cherish.

The time in the bonding room has its potential difficulties, too. It's possible for you to be so engrossed in your new baby that you forget to pay attention to your wife.[1] Several of the wives in my research were angry at being ignored during their husbands' visits, since the husbands seemed to focus entirely on the babies. One of the fathers said to me:

> "I just sit here and stare at it and talk to the wife and comfort her a bit. But the main thing is the baby. I just want to hold the baby."

Remembering that this is a process that the two of you have shared together may help you to keep your perspective. Then, too, just having some understanding of the process of engrossment will prepare you to cope with it so that you can give nurturing and support to your wife while continuing to respond to the baby.

It's important for you to understand something else that your wife is going through now. With the delivery of the baby, your wife has literally given something up.[2] She has lost something precious to her. She has experienced the termination of the ultimate biological bond, the physical union between mother and fetus. Never again will she have the same degree of closensss with her child. There is a feeling of sadness at this loss, and it is absolutely essential that this sense of something being taken away be balanced by taking the newborn baby into her arms. As she touches and explores the infant, she begins to experience a new link with her child.

As a father you've had a different experience, a different relationship with your unborn child. During the pregnancy your wife's abdomen was a wall between you and the fetus. So your own task of hooking up with the infant now may be easier than hers, for rather than losing something, you have gained something.

Some parents want to share this time in the bonding room, or even share the birth itself, with other family members or intimate friends. This may be possible if you have had a home delivery or delivery in a flexible hospital or alternate birth center. It can be a joyous experience for everyone. One grandparent described his feelings of exhilaration at seeing his daughter give birth to his first grandchild: "It was the most incredible sight I've ever seen. I felt delirious with joy. I felt reborn!"

One mother said that her four-year-old daughter had witnessed the birth of her second child and later bragged in school, "I saw my sister born. She came out of my mommy's vagina." As a result, she was very close to her little sister, wanting to touch and hold her constantly.

One word of caution, however. If siblings are to be present at the birth, they need to be prepared in advance. They also need to have an adult with them constantly during the labor and delivery, to explain what's happening and give them reassurance. Even so, they may still be fearful when they see their mother experiencing the pain of labor contractions, or at the sight of blood during the actual birth. An open-door policy is essential for the children, allowing them to leave when their anxiety level is too high and return when they feel more comfortable. They should never be forced to be present.

Your older children can also be present during the family-bonding time. All of you together can experience the charged excitement, the afterglow of intimacy that pervades the atmosphere. As you embrace, hug, and cuddle one another, you can help them to achieve an experience of closeness with their newborn sibling. Urge them to touch and explore the baby's body, just as you yourself do. Talk to them about the baby, about her eyes, her soft skin, her tiny features. Point out different aspects of her behavior. In this way your children are more likely to feel that they too have gained something, a little brother or sister who is now a part of their lives.

Although grandparents are invariably moved by the birth and the bonding experience, they are frequently concerned that they may be treading on your territory, especially after the birth. You or your wife may need to take the initiative by offering the baby to them. However, it should be understood that you and your wife and child will eventually want time alone to get to know one another.

The first two hours after the birth are an especially important time for you to make contact with the baby. She is more active and alert then than she will be in subsequent hours.[3] She has a tremendous impact on everyone around her. Her alertness and activity make you acutely aware that she is a human being with a personality all her own. She pulls you in and forces you to make contact.

The bonding room experience has a kind of energy of its own, generated by the coming together of your little family. Your child's presence is a confirmation that the two of you have weathered a powerful storm, gone through a unique life process together. The period in the bonding room is a culmination of all that has happened, a bonding not only to the baby, but also between you and your wife, leading to a new dimension of your marital vessel.

·5·

The Hospital: Asserting Your Needs

The hospital experience can have a dramatic impact on your emerging new family, and this impact can be either positive or negative.

In some hospitals, the staff are very nurturing and responsive to parents' needs. At times they can provide just that extra encouragement at the right time, to help bring the father into relationship with his wife and child. When an intervention by medical or nursing staff results in a father's presence at the birth, it can have far-ranging implications. This is clearly seen in these words of a first-time English father:

> "I didn't plan on being in the delivery room. I didn't go to any of the father evenings. I didn't want anybody telling me what to do. But when my wife called and said she was going into the hospital, I came on in. When I got there, I peeked in through one of those windows in the door and I could see that she was already in the delivery room. It was then that a nurse asked me if I'd like to go in and I said, 'Yes, thank you, don't mind if I do.' I'm quite sure that if she hadn't asked me at that moment, I wouldn't have thought to go in. I didn't plan to. But at that point it just felt like the most natural thing in the world. I was with my wife and saw my child being born. It was the most incredible sight. I wouldn't have missed it for the world. I felt ten feet tall, just ten feet tall. Any father who wouldn't be affected would

> have to be crazy, wouldn't he? . . . I'm still high. I'm for sure going to be there for the next one."

In another situation, a physician was extremely responsive to a father who was initially fearful of being present at the birth. His fears were the result of having been present as a child, without support, when his mother was giving birth at home. His mother had been unprepared. He had heard her screams and thought she was dying. He commented:

> "I wasn't all that caught up about going into the delivery room. I just didn't have any good reason to go in there. I thought I'd let the professionals get on with it and when everything was okay I would come back. The doctor didn't pressure me. He tried to persuade me. I said, 'No, I really don't think so.' He said, 'Why don't you come in?' I said I would come in if I could leave whenever I felt like it. He said, 'Sure.' I left when she started pushing."

With the doctor's encouragement, this father returned and witnessed his baby's birth. He felt swept off his feet. He was captivated by his newborn's presence and felt extremely close to his wife and child.

The period immediately before the birth and several months afterward is a time of crisis for your emerging family. As in all crises, significant emotional growth and positive change are possible. In the presence of a supportive, concerned hospital staff, the initial coming together of your family can be a positive, fruitful event. If the hospital's attitude toward you, the father, is one of respect and concern for your feelings, you are much more likely to feel like an integral part of the whole family from the beginning.

Despite the increasing popularity of home deliveries, it is still within the hospital that most families come together for the first time. The hospital is thus often the first social institution that a new family has contact with. As such, it is a culture carrier that informs you of society's attitudes and expectations. Concretely, then, for you as a new father, it can give the message, "Be involved with your infant; you are an important member of the family. Your wife and child need you."

An increasing number of hospitals have become sensitive to the needs of parents and encourage father participation in labor and delivery. However, there are still hospitals that, without realizing it, encourage fathers to blunt their feelings toward their babies. They do this by denying that the father exists. Would you believe that even now, in our enlightened age, there are still many hospitals in the Western world that regard the notion of a father's presence in the delivery room with disapproval? Even when the father is present, he may be ignored or treated as an intruder, and the newborn may not be offered to him. The notion of family bonding and the opportunity for the whole family to be together for several hours immediately after the birth may be entirely neglected.

In such a hospital the father is often viewed as coming from the outside and therefore unsterile. Although he may be allowed to visit in his wife's room for several hours during the day, he is usually asked to leave when the baby is brought in. He finally gets to see his infant in the observation window of the nursery. But he can't touch him. He is separated by a glass curtain that leaves him tantalized by the sight of his child, and frustrated by his inability to make contact with him. When he is finally permitted to be with the baby, he is often limited to one hour per day. His wife fares little better, for she may be permitted to be with the infant only every three or four hours for feeding. Small wonder that parents in those circumstances are in such a hurry to get home with their baby.

An outsider looking in might readily assume that this hospital policy is designed to isolate the father from his wife and child, to encourage him to deny the birth experience and the existence of his baby and thus gradually become detached from the family unit. If the destruction of the family was the hospital's goal, it would be hard to imagine its being accomplished more effectively.

In my own case, I was able to be alone with my wife and baby for only about ten minutes immediately following the birth. Then Jonathan was whisked away to the nursery. Claudia and I experienced a keen sense of frustration and disappointment at not having more time with our baby. I felt driven to make contact with him as soon as possible, and Claudia encouraged me to do so. That contact came one hour later during the hospital's visiting period, when I had to work my way through the throng of people milling about in front of the glass wall of the nursery. I saw Jonathan and, my nose pressed to the glass, I took my first pictures of him as I tried to talk to him. "Hi, Jonathan. This is your daddy. You sure are beautiful." The opportunity to see him was fleeting, however, because he was soon wheeled away again. I wanted to hold him, but I was grateful to have had at least a glimpse of him.

Five hours after the birth, Jonathan was brought into Claudia's room for the first time. But the nurse became alarmed when she saw me and asked me to leave. She said that fathers were not allowed in the same room with the babies on the first night after the birth—hospital policy. It was only after I made a special request of the head nurse that I was allowed to stay with them for twenty minutes. It wasn't as much time as we wanted, but at least it was something.

I was happy that I had not given up when the nurse told me to leave, and I felt grateful to the supervisor for granting my request. It was only later that I asked myself why it should have been so difficult to spend a small period of time with my wife and child. Why should it be such a big deal for us to be together as a family?

Since then, in talking with other new parents, I've heard many stories about the frustration and anger they've experienced in trying to get the hospital to meet their needs. This seemed to occur even in hospitals where fathers were allowed to be present in the labor and delivery rooms. Some fathers felt that they were in the way at the hospital or did not have the right to express their wishes. Several were reluctant to talk about their experiences, indicating there was no use, nothing could be done.

Their anger was often related to (1) situations when their wives were in pain or required immediate care and there was no response from the medical or nursing staff; (2) inadequate explanations or none at all, sometimes because of insufficient time; (3) procedures planned or carried out without their being consulted; or (4) rudeness or downright hostility by hospital staff, either to them or their wives. In all of these situations the fathers felt out of control. In one instance, a father insisted that his wife was about to deliver. Since he was a first-time father, the nursing staff assumed that he was being hysterical and told him to calm down. Too late they realized that the father had good reason for concern. His wife wound up delivering in the hallway. As you can imagine, this father felt frustrated and helpless with the staff's indifference to his appeals, and every time he thought about this later he became enraged.

The crisis of birth and delivery is foreign territory, where you must rely upon others for your wife's and later your child's welfare. Your wife is facing her internal world: the toil of labor and the pain of her contractions, pain that can be minimized with training but is nevertheless often present. That leaves you to be her mediator, her buffer with the external world, her protector. In her preoccupation with labor she may be unaware of unresponsive care, slights, and insensitive comments, or she may just not have the energy to react to them. She may expect you to protect her, but you may feel impotent against this powerful institutional structure. It can be bitterly frustrating.

You can become preoccupied with your anger to the extent that it interferes with your excitement and happiness at the birth. If you express your anger and it distracts your wife from her own happiness and bonding, you may both become upset. The presence of the baby triggers such positive, nurturing feelings that it is hard for her to feel angry at other things that may be going on around her. Perhaps this difficulty in expressing anger is also a self-preservation mechanism. She feels weak and dependent upon hospital staff, and she may fear that expressions of anger will result in retaliation against her. Thus her anger is covered over and denied or, if felt, relegated to a position of nonimportance.

My wife felt this way. Even during the first few hours at the hospital I was angry at the staff's insensitive treatment of Claudia, but I tried to mute my gradually rising anger because I was afraid it would interfere with our primary goal of delivering a healthy baby.

I began to get mad during the labor because of numerous incidents that showed a lack of regard for our feelings. On one occasion a nurse asked to examine Claudia while she was having a contraction, and I motioned for her to wait. She stood there, arms akimbo, a scowl on her face, her foot lightly tapping the floor, and commented, "Through now?"

"I was having a contraction," my wife said weakly.

The nurse replied acidly, "That's exactly when I wanted to examine you."

I could have handled the arbitrary hospital rules, any one or even a few of these insensitive incidents could have been overlooked and forgotten. But these caregivers behaved as if they were at war and my wife and I were the enemy. There was no end to the things that contributed to my anger and could have spoiled the marvelousness of the birth experience for me if I had allowed it to. And all of this was happening in a hospital that encouraged father participation. "I should try to put this out of my head," I told myself. "A new father shouldn't feel angry, he should feel happy and overjoyed." And I did feel that, but I still couldn't make the anger go away. From the research I had done in numerous maternity hospitals, I knew that it was possible for parents to be treated with respect and dignity, so it was especially hard for me to swallow this kind of treatment.

It's possible that your own experience with the hospital and its staff may be a positive one, and as hospitals become increasingly responsive to parents' needs, the likelihood of this occurring will increase. But what if your experience is negative, while your wife, in contrast, seems filled with feelings of joy? Expressing your rage may make you feel better, but it will also destroy your wife's elation. She is likely to feel angry at you for dissipating her "high." Not a very good way to get started. So wait until later and share these feelings with one of your friends, one who has recently become a father. Another father will understand what you're going through, and you will find it extremely helpful to let off some steam with him. Later, when you and your wife are talking about your respective experiences at the hospital, you can share some of your earlier feelings of frustration and anger.

Once your wife and baby are home, you can also express your anger at your treatment by sending a letter to the hospital administration. This will allow you to vent your feelings at a time when your wife is no longer dependent on the hospital and thus feeling vulnerable and open to attack. Not only will writing this letter make you feel better, but it can have a significant impact on the hospital. First of all, your wife's physician will probably be delighted, particularly if he has been frustrated in his efforts to encourage the hospital staff to be more responsive to new families. Documenting your concerns, your anger at the way you and your wife were treated, gives him something concrete to use in his struggles with the hospital.

Your letter also counters a tactic often used by the hospital bureaucracy: "We have no evidence *in writing* to show any problems or concerns on the part of our patients." When expressions of outrage are received from a great many parents, the pressure on the hospital to change becomes overwhelming.

♦ Creating a Better Experience for Yourself

The hospital has always been on hallowed ground, immune from criticism. Its rules and procedures are said to be for the good of the child and the mother. So sometimes even shabby treatment is tolerated, perhaps expected. A new father, frustrated by his inability to visit his wife and baby together after the birth, commented:

> "That's the way it is. I just kind of accepted it. You can't fight society. Can't fight the hospital. They know what they're doing."

This is the ultimate in socialization. And it impresses the new family with feelings of being uncared for, isolated, and detached from one another. As a result, the husband and wife sometimes make each other the receptacle for all their frustration and rage. This can be a significant barrier for the new emerging family to overcome.

This need not be your family's experience of the hospital, however. There are many ways of preparing yourself to participate in the birth experience as fully as you would like, and of asserting yourself with the hospital. Nothing can guarantee the goodwill and support of all of the staff, but certainly you needn't passively accept hospital procedures if they interfere with the bonding of your family. In fact, it's amazing how much flexibility is inherent in even the most rigid hospital procedures once you begin to ask questions and assert your needs.

In the past, some fathers have dramatically demonstrated their need to be with their family during the birth and immediately afterward. In 1964, at a time when the California Department of Public Health was debating the enforcement of a law that would exclude fathers from the delivery room, one father handcuffed himself to his laboring wife and threw the key away so that there was no way he would be excluded.[1]

More recently, another father of my acquaintance demonstrated another way. He had been present at the birth, felt engrossed in his child, and was extremely protective of him. When the nursing staff arrived to carry out the routine laboratory procedures, he said that he wanted to remain with his child. They were somewhat surprised.

"You want to stay? Why? We're going to stick him, he'll feel pain." The father replied, "That's all right. I want to be there. I want to be able to hold him and hug him and talk to him when he cries and is in pain." This unnerved the health-care personnel somewhat, because they had never had a father assert himself to this degree. Nevertheless, the father was insistent and he had his way.

When the baby was finally taken back to the nursery, the father again refused to leave his child's side. And once again the nursing staff, to their credit, acquiesced. He cuddled and cooed to his infant and later spoke with pride about how he had been immediately available when his child needed him.

These dramatic responses demonstrate the depth of some fathers' need to be a part of the unfolding process of birth and delivery, to be close to their newborns after the birth. Nowadays such strong protests are usually unnecessary. There are simpler, more straightforward ways of asserting your needs. First, and most important, you can choose your doctor and your hospital.

♦ Choosing Your Doctor and Your Hospital

A genuine choice of hospital experience has not always been readily available. It is really only an enlightened few caregivers who, for largely humanitarian reasons, have been in the vanguard of attempting to make hospitals not only accountable for providing good medical care but also for being sensitive to the bonding process of the entire family. Because of these efforts they have at times been subjected to ridicule and even ostracism by their professional colleagues. To name only a few of these fine doctors we would have to include Robert Bradley in Denver, John Miller in San Francisco, Marshall Klaus in Cleveland and Lansing, Michigan, John Kennell in Cleveland, T. Berry Brazelton in Boston, Norman Morris in London, and Pierre Vellay in Paris. Furthermore, the work of Frederick Leboyer and his concept of "birth without violence" have forced us to take a second look at the conditions surrounding the birth of a baby.[2] In addition, we owe a great debt of gratitude to the work of several others who are now deceased. These include Grantley Dick-Read in England, who developed the idea of natural childbirth; Ferdinand Lamaze in France, who pioneered the notion of painless childbirth and the "Lamaze Method"; Edith Jackson of

New Haven and Denver, who pioneered modern-day rooming-in; and finally, John Lind in Stockholm, Sweden, who emphasized the importance of the father's early participation with the baby.[3]

Recently hospitals, in response to their increasing financial crunch, have been forced to reevaluate attitudes and inaugurate procedures to appeal to and attract more patients. Parents have begun to stop using those hospitals that were found to be insensitive to their needs. You have the ultimate power, the power of the pocketbook. And as you begin to talk with your wife, the two of you will gradually develop a shared view of how you want the birth experience to be. Ask yourselves, "What do we each want out of the childbirth experience?" You can decide whether you'd like the birth to occur in the hospital, at home, or in an alternate birth center (sometimes located in a separate clinic, but often part of a hospital). And if you select a hospital, it will be one that you've actively sought out, one that is responsive to you and your wife's notion of the degree of participation you want.

The choice you make will also depend upon the community you live in. If you are in an urban area, you will usually have the greatest selection. Most likely there will be a number of hospitals that encourage father participation during the delivery and allow bonding time following the birth. There will probably be one or more alternate birth centers and perhaps a birth clinic as well. And, although it's uncommon, you may even be able to find a doctor who does home deliveries.

If you live in a rural area, your options will be limited. Often there is only one hospital serving a small community, and more often than not that hospital will not have an alternate birth center affiliated with it. In addition, it will be a rare occurrence to find a doctor who is willing to do a home delivery, although in some rural communities doctors do home deliveries out of necessity.

However, if there is a university hospital within striking distance, you may find new opportunities available for participation in the birth experience. Some parents who live in rural areas drive as far as one hundred miles and more to be able to have the kind of experience they want. They have strong feelings about this, and they're willing to go to great lengths in order to get what they want. Sometimes they go to live with friends or relatives shortly before the birth so they'll be closer to the hospital or clinic of their choice.

If your local hospital permits only limited contact among mother, father, and baby, and you have no other alternatives, you and your wife may want to consider having her and the baby discharged within twenty-four hours. Many doctors permit and support this, and of course sometimes it must be done because of a family's limited financial resources.

Many parents who are concerned about the shortcomings of hospitals still choose to have their baby delivered there because they fear something may go wrong in a home delivery. In Holland, however, a country where home deliveries are common, infant mortality is among the lowest in the world.[4] In one section of the United States (Marin County, California), home deliveries now constitute 7.6 percent of the births and no increased risk has been noted.[5] However, a drawback to home births in the United States is the sparcity of physicians who are willing to participate as well as the lack of trained midwives. In addition, because of resistance in the medical community, there is often difficulty in coordinating backup emergency hospital care, which increases the risk in complicated births.

You may be uncertain as to how to get the information you need in order to make a decision about a doctor and a hospital. Basically, you'll get it by talking to people. Speak with your family doctor about what you and your wife are hoping for in the birth experience. Find out what doctors he recommends, and ask him which hospitals would even allow what you're asking for. Talk to friends who have recently become parents and ask them to tell you about their experience with the hospital and the doctor. Find out who their childbirth educators were and talk to them. If your wife has a good rapport with her gynecologist, his name should probably go at the top of the list.

The crucial step will be to make your wishes about the birth clear in the interview with the physician. You will want to know if he will allow you to be present in the delivery room. Clearly, if he does not and you feel strongly that you wish to be present, then you and your wife will have to work with another doctor. It's either that or give up something that will be very important and meaningful to you.

Many doctors, given prodding, will allow fathers to participate in the delivery room. Some are more understanding and accepting of this than others. For example, when one young mother-to-be said she wished her husband to be present at the birth, her physician replied, "I can do without him." She insisted, "But I really want him there. It's important for me."

At this her doctor said, "Okay, I can do without him, but if you really want him there it's okay with me."

Another doctor once remarked to me, "Personally, I don't think it makes a difference—fathers in the delivery room holding the baby, all this bonding stuff. That's just a few hours. You can't tell me that's more important than all that goes afterward. Anyway, I don't care; if that's what parents want I'll give it to them."

Another doctor, in a joking comment, told a mother-to-be, "If you want to have your baby riding down Fifth Avenue on the back of a horse, we'll do it."

Find out if your doctor is interested in facilitating bonding, not only between mother and baby but also between father and baby. Ask him whether he gives the baby to both father and mother after the birth. Does he allow the mother to put the baby to breast? If your baby is in good health, will you and your wife be allowed to hold the baby most of the time in the delivery room, or will it need to be in an isolette, separated from you? Notice whether the doctor talks directly to you at the interview and lets you know that he appreciates your presence and comments on how important this is for your wife. Notice whether he encourages your participation and feedback and urges your presence at your wife's prenatal visits and childbirth education classes.

It is also important to know whether the doctor allows you to be present in the operating room, should your wife require a cesarean section. Anywhere from ten to twenty percent of women are delivered by cesarean section, depending on the hospital, the geographical area, and the physician.[6] So it is always a possibility, although many parents are reluctant to think about it in advance. Some doctors are now allowing fathers to be present during a C-section if they attend cesarean birth preparation classes. A doctor's willingness to do this shows an extremely flexible attitude toward fathers and families.

Ask the doctor about the rules and regulations at the hospital he uses. For example, to participate in the delivery room, you will almost always need to attend a series of childbirth education lectures. This is a standard practice that is of immeasurable benefit. Ask whether the hospital has an alternate birth center. Find out whether the hospital permits you and your wife to be alone with your baby for at least two hours after the birth. Find out whether there are hospital rules that prevent you from holding your baby immediately after the birth. Find out whether you can have skin-to-skin contact with your baby and whether this is something the doctor encourages. In some hospitals fathers are allowed to take off their shirts and hold the baby directly against their body, a delightful experience that has previously been open only to mothers.[7]

Find out how soon you and your wife can be with your baby again after he is taken to the nursery. Most hospitals limit the parents' contact with the baby immediately after the birth, some for as much as twenty-four hours, saying they need to observe the infant. This period of time is completely arbitrary, and if the baby is healthy there is no reason why it should be so long. It will be important for you to make it known that if the hour is reasonable, you would like to be able to visit *together* with your wife and child, perhaps within six hours after the birth. This should clearly be in addition to the immediate bonding time of at least two hours.

♦ Rooming-In

Find out whether the infant can stay with your wife throughout the day, which is called rooming-in. There are different varieties of rooming-in. Sometimes the baby is with the mother from about nine to five (or nine to nine), and then is returned to the nursery. In other situations, the baby is constantly in the room with his mother and sleeps there also. Usually, however, even in the latter situation, the mother may ask to have the baby returned to the nursery for a period of time if she feels she wants the rest or would like to go for a walk. You'll need to ask how soon after the birth the baby can be placed in the room. This can vary from nearly immediately to twenty-four hours, depending upon the hospital.

I strongly urge you to use rooming-in if the hospital has it. Rooming-in has significant advantages for the father, for fathers almost always have virtually unlimited visiting privileges in facilities like these. This environment has such a positive effect on fathers' feelings toward their newborn babies that early researchers wanted to call these facilities "rooming-in units for parents and newborns."[8] In addition, the visiting policy for other family members is usually much more flexible in these units. And of course, rooming-in has significant advantages for the mother. My own research in Sweden confirmed other studies to the effect that women who room-in with their babies feel much more confident and competent about themselves as mothers. These mothers also had a greater understanding of their babies' behavior, which made them feel they needed less help at home. In addition, there is an increased incidence of breast feeding among rooming-in mothers.[9] And the opportunity for father, mother, and baby to be together throughout the day probably enhances bonding among all of them. Dr. Marshall Klaus observed that the opportunity for mothers to have increased contact with their babies during the first days after birth dramatically enhances bonding;[10] recent research suggests that this is true of fathers as well.[11]

In order to get rooming-in, you will need to request it early since there may be only one room designated for this. Generally speaking, if your wife does not have rooming-in or use alternate birth facilities, the baby is kept in the nursery and brought in to her room every four hours. Whether or not you are allowed to be present then will depend on the hospital's policy. The most rigid hospital policy forbids fathers from having contact with the baby. This was common twenty years ago but is less the case today. More commonly, fathers are allowed to be present one or more times during the day when the baby is brought in from the nursery.

♦ Sibling Visits

If you have one or more small children at home, it is essential to know the hospital's policy on their visiting. Research indicates that siblings make a much better adjustment to the newborn if they have an opportunity to visit the hospital, see their mother and father, and become gradually acclimatized to the newborn baby.[12] Are siblings permitted in the room with the baby? Are they permitted to hold the baby? If siblings are not permitted in your wife's room, is there any objection to her taking the baby to see them in a hospital waiting room? Unfortunately, many hospitals still do not allow children to visit in the room unless they are over fourteen. However, there is usually a conference room or a waiting room that can be set aside for your younger children to see their mother and to get acquainted with their new baby brother or sister. This is not ideal, but at least it is something. You will want to know exactly what the policy is so you can prepare your children for their part in this experience.

♦ Alternate Birth Center

An alternate birth center is essentially an extremely flexible rooming-in unit. Labor and birth may both take place in the room, and it is usually decorated in a homelike fashion. Siblings and other extended family members are sometimes allowed to be present at the birth. Afterward, the baby stays in the room throughout the day and fathers have unlimited visiting privileges. Again, if you are using a hospital, you'll have to request the alternate birth center in advance because there may be only one or two rooms designated for this.

♦ Sibling at the Birth

If you and your wife have selected an alternate birth center or home delivery and are even remotely considering a sibling's participation at the birth, you will want to know your doctor's attitude toward this. If he considers it a possibility, then you'll both want to discuss it with your youngster in advance, but without insisting that he make a decision right away. If he wants to learn more about what the experience might be, you could include him in the childbirth classes and your wife's prenatal visits to the doctor, just as if he were going to participate in the birth. His interest may increase over the nine months of pregnancy, just as you yourself become more focused on the event with the passage of each trimester.

If your child does participate, the supportive adult at his side during labor and delivery should be someone other than you. You will be too intent on your wife and the new baby to be aware of your other child's needs. And as I mentioned earlier, he should be able to leave and reenter the room as his anxiety dictates. More research needs to be done on the impact of the birth on siblings. Klaus and Kennell, although permitting children's presence during labor and shortly after birth, discourage their presence at the birth itself out of concern that children, especially younger children may be confused by some of the procedures and also because it is difficult to evaluate what the experience has meant to the child.[13]

♦ Hospital Attitude

Throughout the entire process it is important to remember that despite your doctor's philosophical orientation, he may not be able to alter established hospital procedures. This is why you must inquire not only about his views but also about the actual practice in the hospital he works with.

It would be helpful to know whether your doctor's hospital has a humanitarian and progressive attitude only on paper or whether its staff really practice what they preach. To this end, and also to prepare yourself, you and your wife should visit the hospital beforehand. This, by the way, is usually done in association with most childbirth education classes. At the hospital, an easy way to determine the sensitivity and responsiveness of the staff is to observe the way they answer questions. Ask them how they feel about fathers in the delivery room and about family bonding. If they show some enthusiasm that's a good sign.

As parents-to-be you have a right to ask questions about a hospital, to learn about its orientation, and to receive clarification about uncertainties you may have about treatment. If people (your doctor or the hospital staff) take the time to explain and reassure you, if they are friendly and treat you with respect, it speaks well for the doctor and the hospital. However, if they seem abrupt, short-tempered, and condescending, and give you the impression that they think you're an idiot for asking any questions at all, then seek a more positive climate elsewhere.

♦ Making Your Decisions Work

You and your wife need to focus on such questions as the amount and type of pain relief she wants, whether immediate bonding time is desired, whether rooming-in is to be requested, and if so whether the baby is to be present just during the day or on a twenty-four-hour basis. In addition, your wife may have other, more detailed requests relative to her delivery, and the two of you may have specific requests about how you want your baby treated immediately after the birth, assuming that everything goes normally. Type up a list of your requests and make ten copies. Give them to your doctors, nurses, and any other caregivers who may be around at the time you and your wife enter the hospital. Typing it up helps, because in addition to being easier to read, it looks more official. Anything that looks official is more likely to be carried out by hospital personnel. This means you will interact with them in a more positive way because your needs are being met.

You'll also be much more relaxed once you and your wife have organized what you expect of the hospital. And having gotten acknowledgment from your wife's doctor that he will try to honor your requests, you now have some power and a sense of control of you and your wife's destiny. Then later, if things don't seem to be going according to your requests, you can say something like, "This is different from what we agreed to. Has something happened?"

Things seem to move very rapidly during the latter part of labor. There is a tremendous sense of urgency, and you may fear that something could happen to your wife. Some fathers admit to such fears only afterward, if ever. At such a time, it is very easy to back away and allow the people who are "in the know" to take over. But this is exactly when you need to stand up on your wife's behalf. For example, if she doesn't want extra sedation during labor, you simply say so. Often the woman feels helpless and at the mercy of those assigned to carrying out her care. At such a time it can be easy for her to give up her autonomy and allow the hospital to take over. Small wonder that so many women have wound up accepting sedation. The doctor or nurse's question, "Would you like some pain medicine?" is heard as "Why don't you take some pain medicine. I know what's best for you."

But if you and your wife have discussed the issue of pain relief and how much she feels is appropriate, you can help back her up in her resolve. Your support, concern, and caring at this time will relieve her anxiety, which not only enhances her courage to cope with pain but also tends to decrease the pain.

Another thing that will help you is knowing how to ask questions. First of all, you must be ready to ask your questions when the opportunity arises. Perhaps when you see the doctor he speaks with you briefly, and then comes the inevitable "Any questions?" He waits one and a half seconds and is gone. Afterward you kick yourself for not lunging forward with your questions.

Carry a pen and some index cards with you. When you think of a question, write it on a card and stick it in your front pocket. When the doctor approaches, pull out your cards to remind yourself of the questions and start talking immediately, before he can get away. Say that you have several questions, then briefly state what you want to know.

Some doctors tend to overexplain or oversimplify, failing to recognize that many fathers today are much more educated about the facts of labor and delivery than they were years ago. Simply mention that you are aware of what he is saying and then go on to your area of concern. This gives him a sense of your level of knowledge without setting up an adversary situation. Or your doctor may talk in medical terms and statistics, so you may have to ask, "What does that mean here?" or something like that. Many parents are fearful of appearing "dumb," and even if they don't understand what was said to them, they still nod their heads in the affirmative when asked, "Do you understand?" If you don't understand, have the courage to ask your question again, and rephrase it if you have to. If the doctor heads for the door before he has finished answering something that is important to you, walk alongside him and continue to talk with him.

Once you begin to take charge in this fashion you'll feel better about yourself and your role. It's amazing how one or two brief questions from a father and perhaps five minutes of explanation from the doctor can make the difference between the father's feeling that he's working together with the doctor and the hospital versus feeling that he's being belittled and neglected.

You will need to ask questions of hospital staff too, especially about rules and procedures that seem contrary to your purposes. Never assume that there is a medical reason for a given procedure. The fact is that many standard practices have long since outlived their medical utility. Also, a large proportion of the rules are set up more for the convenience of the hospital than for the good of the parents and their baby. So if you don't like the way something is being done, ask about it. Perhaps it's only a routine, not a medical necessity, and perhaps it can be changed.

Another problem you must confront is that often the hospital staff are well intentioned but rushed, and you just have to be assertive to make sure your requests aren't skipped over. Sometimes things don't seem to go the way they're supposed to simply because of a lack of communication. For example, a young mother told me:

> "When our daughter was born, I had rooming-in and the sign on the door said rooming-in. There were two of us in the room. Every time the shift changed nurses, they would march in and rip those babies out of our hands and throw them into the nursery. Finally we realized that they hadn't read what was on the door and they didn't know. We finally figured out what to do. Every time we saw a new nurse, we would say 'rooming-in.' Then she would say, 'Oh, terrific.' "

I think I should also say something in defense of the nursing profession in general, for I do not mean to malign nurses. The majority of them are well-meaning, talented, hardworking, and conscientious. In fact, one of the problems between nurses and mothers arises out of the nurses' loving feelings for the babies they tend. That problem is competition.

As an intern working on a children's unit, I was aware of an intense competition between nursing staff and mothers. It was as if each was trying to demonstrate who was the best parent. The nursing staff looked forward to seeing "their babies" and loved them dearly. And the parents often felt under attack in front of the nurses. Now that parents are increasingly assuming the care of their babies, nursing staff are being relegated to a secondary role. Instead, they are called upon to provide support and instruction and to back up the new parents in their attempts to care for their youngsters. It may be very hard for some of them to make these changes. Some may feel angry at not being able to nurture and love the babies as they have in the past, for it is a real loss to them. And without realizing exactly why, they may do everything in their power to get the babies back to the nursery.

So keep in mind that some of your problems with nursing staff come about because they really care about the babies. As much as possible, try to foster a friendly rather than competitive atmosphere with the staff. Still, you do have to assert yourself sometimes. One father told me this experience:

> "A nurse came in and announced, "Well, we're taking your baby back to the nursery.' I said, 'But we've got twenty-four-hour rooming-in.' The nurse then said, 'But

you won't be able to have any visitors if he stays.' So I said, 'That's okay. We don't want any visitors anyway.' "

You'll need to assert yourself not only with the staff but also with the hospital machines. Don't assume that because a piece of mechanical equipment is in the picture you have no rights. You have as much right to be at your wife's side as any machine. During Claudia's labor, as I mentioned, monitoring equipment to measure her contractions and the fetal heartbeat was positioned in such a way that it took my place at the bedside. Finally I moved the monitoring equipment and the bed to make room for myself. Afterward, I wondered why they had put the machine there in the first place without suggesting to me how I could sit or even that I could move it. Had they intended to displace me or were they just unthinking or, even worse, just didn't care? After all, I was only a father-to-be, not a patient. From their point of view, maybe I didn't really have any rights. If I hadn't decided to tangle with the monitoring equipment, I would for all practical purposes have been removed from the labor process. This situation, I believe, demonstrates the necessity for interacting with the machines of our technological age. In this way they begin to work for us, rather than displacing and dehumanizing us.

♦ A Premature Birth

If your baby is born prematurely, the necessity for special medical procedures can interfere with the bonding process. But even in this situation, you will still have opportunities for contact. You'll just have to make a greater effort to prevent yourself from feeling detached from your baby. You must immediately let the hospital staff know that you want to be able to hold your baby in the intensive-care-unit nursery. The key word is bonding: "I want to be able to bond to my baby." The staff cannot ignore that, and you and your wife will probably be able to do it. Many medical centers now recognize the importance of parental visits and encourage parents to hold their premature infants right from the beginning.

Fears and misconceptions about a premature birth can hamper the bonding to your youngster. You may think that because he is so tiny you shouldn't touch him. You may fear dislodging some of his monitoring equipment or injuring him in some way. And you may feel a great deal of anxiety at seeing your baby amid this mass of medical machinery. Perhaps you and your wife wonder what you could have done differently to prevent the baby's premature birth, and you may blame yourselves. You expected a full-term, alert baby, and this baby may hardly respond. He is nothing like the image you carried in your mind of what your baby would be like, and you may feel a great sense of sadness. Feeling this way, it would be easy to withdraw and decrease the frequency of your visits. Your withdrawal is one way of expressing your grief. And your grief can function as a wall between you and your baby, preventing you from accepting the child before you. This is precisely why it's so important that you and your wife continue to visit regularly and that both of you hold the baby as often as possible even though he is in the intensive-care nursery.

Often the nursing staff regard the premature babies with even greater affection than usual, an affection born of frequent and close contact with them during their day-to-day care. They're very involved with your baby and can be extremely supportive of your efforts. So try to set up a situation where you and the staff are working together. A climate of mutual support can help in your bonding to your baby, and since you won't fear that the nurses are critical of your efforts, you'll feel more comfortable about asking for their help.

♦ Fathers of the World, Unite!

Hospitals, and for that matter our culture at large, have in the past treated fathers-to-be like buffoons. Cartoons have portrayed us as inadequate and scatterbrained. This is clearly seen in depictions of fathers on their way to the maternity hospital with their wives. They are shown marching out of the house without their pants, or getting lost, or running out of gas. Hospitals used to assume that we would either faint or become hysterical at the first sight of blood. As a result, we were excluded from the birth process. And we ourselves acquiesced in this viewpoint of ourselves and even believed it at times.

It's about time this point of view were changed. But it's not likely to be altered if we sit back on our haunches and allow ourselves to be treated as if we didn't exist. It may be up to you to take the first steps in bringing about friendly cooperation among you, your doctor, and the hospital staff. This kind of cooperative attitude now exists in many hospitals but still not all. And if the cooperation isn't there, then you must simply assert yourself. You do have rights. This is your baby; the hospital doesn't own him. So speak up. Your voice counts, and you can have a great deal of impact. Although you are striving for cooperation, you must be willing to confront and alter the often rigid and inflexible attitudes of that most powerful institution that new fathers first have contact with: the maternity hospital.

·6·

Good-bye to Childhood

My son was born at 4:22 in the afternoon on June 11, 1974. As I reflected back from that moment it was hard to believe that only ten hours and twenty-two minutes had elapsed from the time Claudia had first aroused me on that special day. It seemed like an eternity—so much had happened. I wasn't just ten and a half hours older, I was suddenly months and years older. I had gone from being a boy to a man in one fell swoop. And with my child's birth I was suddenly brought face to face with my own mortality. I felt I was now not only older but suddenly more mature, one step further along the path of my own life, and thus one step closer to my own death.

Parenthood universally alters the way in which we view ourselves and the world around us. With this event, a man now views himself less as a son in relation to his own parents and more as a father in relation to his own child. With fatherhood, we have taken a quantum leap forward, not only in terms of our own psychological growth but also in terms of living out our life cycle. The birth of our first child signals that we have less time than we realized.

As children we projected not only age but strength and wisdom on our own fathers. This father image we now place upon ourselves, with all of its accompanying energy and power. And we feel the ties of our childhood loosening as we perceive ourselves passing suddenly from boyhood to manhood.

The intense emotions you experienced at the birth, as well as your new sense of yourself and your world, may leave you struggling to comprehend your new situation. You may have trouble believing what has happened. Like me you may ask yourself several times, "Am I really a father?" And each time the response is, "Yes, I'm a father, I really am a father."

I had a hard time grasping the full implication of those words. I was now a father in relation to my own child. And since this was so, did that then mean that I was no longer a son in relation to my own father? It was still difficult to take it all in. Sometimes I even wondered who had really been born. For I fantasized that this was my own birth, that I was switching places with my infant son. Of course, this was in many ways also a birth process for me; it was my own birth as a father.

I often found myself thinking, "I am a father and yet that has not really happened. I have a son and yet I am a little boy myself. Images of my own father flashed before my eyes. First I saw myself playing ball with him, then swimming together. Then there were bits and pieces of memories that were hard to grasp. Then a particularly vivid image overtook me. I was four years old, living in New York City. My father was taking us on an outing to relieve my mother of the rigors of childcare. There we were—my three-year-old sister, my father, and I—riding the subway. I grabbed the functionless wheel located in the lead car and pretended that I was steering the train. Then we took the ferry boat to Staten Island, where I saw a whole new world: fishermen laying their traps for the most enormous crabs and lobsters I had ever seen. I remembered the sun so vividly, those enormous crabs, the rocks that jutted out from the shoreline, and the feeling of closeness I had with my father.

I had another vivid image of my father running beside me. I was seven years old, now living with my parents in California. He was teaching me to ride a bicycle. He huffed and puffed as he raced along beside me, pushing my bicycle down the alleyway and stabilizing me as I struggled to keep the bike upright. There came a point when it seemed that his presence and my union with the bicycle had become one. I will never forget that. I assumed he was still pushing me when all of a sudden I heard my dad's voice from fifty yards back, "You're riding, Marty!" he shouted. "You did it!"

"But I'm afraid!" I shouted back as the bicycle moved forward.

"You can do it!" he cried back. "You don't need me anymore. You can do it on your own." And his voice trailed off as I left him far behind.

The images captured the closeness that I have with my father and yet the reality that I was leaving him behind, that I was moving on to a new phase of my life. My recollection of my father running beside me filled me with a need to be near my own child, to be a part of his life, recognizing nevertheless that at one point he would also leave me behind.

I believe it is a universal experience that the power and stress of the birth not only makes us think more about ourselves as parents but also leads us to reexperience our own parents and our own childhood. It is as if the very realization that we are moving forward into a new phase of our lives simultaneously thrusts us backward, resulting in a flood of images and memories from the past. It is as if this were a final glimpse, a last peek into the valley of our youth before we step over the mountain crest into the undeveloped wilderness of parenthood and adulthood. There is a sense of saying good-bye to our childhood as we move into this new stage of our lives. And there is an experience of both joy and sadness in thus moving on.

In these images are also the seeds of your wishes for your own child and for yourself as a father. If your childhood was happy, these images fill you with pleasure, and you wish that your own child could feel the same way about you, his father. But if yours was not a happy childhood and you did not know your father because of death or abandonment, or loss of contact through divorce or because he was simply unavailable, these emotion-laden images can fill you with a great sense of loss. For your child's birth is a reminder that a chapter in your own life is now being closed, and the love you have always wanted from your own father you somehow sense you will now never receive. Seeing your newborn before you reminds you even more of that which you missed in childhood. It is as if that child becomes yourself, and you experience with greater sadness the losses of the past. If that old relationship was characterized by abuse or neglect, the sadness is also mingled with tremendous rage.

Small wonder, then, that you become fearful, anxious, or depressed. You fear being close to your child, because it brings you closer to the losses of your past. You may even feel that you don't know how to be a father. You feel lost, without a guide to show you the way. The territory of fatherhood is still barren and uncharted. You fear leaving your own childhood behind.

This is a crucial period for you as a father, for the images you have about the kind of father you want to be are the images you are most likely to enact. Your decision to make yourself an ongoing part of your child's life will be instrumental throughout his development. You have the capacity to set up patterns of caring and closeness that will become dominant themes in your life as a father and in your relationship with your child. It is important that you start this from birth, from the beginning.

7

Coming Home: Early Struggles

> "Now that I'm used to the idea of having a baby son I can sit down and think of what must be done, step by step. The way seems to be a lot clearer. It's not clogged with obstacles as it was before. Before, I was far too excited, too emotional to do anything. But I feel as though I can get on with these things now."
>
> —Words of a first-time father
> one week after his son's birth.

You will experience a keen sense of relief at having your whole family home together with you for the first time. Yet you may still be feeling a sense of unreality and disbelief that you are really a father. You may ask yourself, "What's my role? Where do I fit in? Is this really happening to me?" It's hard to believe that so much has changed in such a short time.

For several days you may still feel different, perhaps dazed and off kilter. Perhaps you have a hard time gathering your thoughts, as this father did:

> "Everything seemed faster. People seemed to be moving faster or at least I seemed to be moving faster than people around me. My thoughts were all coming at the same time."

It is easy to understand why you felt dazed while your wife and baby were still in the hospital. But you may be perplexed now when your sense of anxiety and unreality intermittently continues after you bring your family home.

The day I drove my wife and son home from the hospital, I felt as if I were floating around in an unanchored state. Everything seemed strange, new, and different. Colors were deeper and more intense. I felt like I was suddenly seeing things for the first time. First it was a tree here, then a house over there, then the view of a whole hillside that I had never noticed before. Later that night when Jonathan cried at two in the morning, I dimly remember waking and thinking, "There's really no baby in the house, I must be dreaming," and going back to sleep as Claudia got up to feed him.

But it's not a dream. And as your sense of unreality persists, you may begin to feel a kind of isolation and confusion about your role now that your baby is home. What do you do as a father? Of course your work is an important contribution, but you did that before. So what will you do differently now? Don't be alarmed at your feelings. This is simply a confusing time, when your senses and even your view of the world are in disarray. It takes some getting used to. If you begin to understand some of these changes, however, this stage will not seem so overwhelming. The experience of disorganization usually subsides within a week or two after the birth, and you soon find yourself back down to earth again.

♦ Finding Your Anchor

A number of factors can speed up or slow down the resolution of these early struggles. Your experiences during the birth and with the hospital are a major factor. It will help if you felt like an involved participant, were able to be present at the birth, had immediate bonding time with your family, ready access to them during visits, and felt that hospital staff were supportive.

Involving yourself in specific activities at home will also help you to retain your sense of reality. For example, a simple activity like sending out the baby announcements with your wife can help. The announcements are a way of stating with pride, "We're parents. Look at us. I'm a father—look at me. We have a son," or "We have a daughter. Isn't she beautiful, and look at how much she weighs and how tall she is.'' The announcements are also a way to reestablish relationships with friends with whom you have lost contact, as you now reach out to the world through your little baby. Affirming to others, ''I'm a father,'' makes you feel more natural in this role.

Perhaps you took pictures of your wife and baby while they were in the hospital. If not, take some now. Send them out with your announcements. Start a baby scrapbook. Fathers tend to let their wives take over this task. Don't! This is a unique opportunity that you can share. Working on the scrapbook will help you experience your newborn in a new way, enhancing your early adjustment.

The scrapbook becomes even more important if you have a premature baby, or a sick baby, or a baby that is in some way different than you expected. Parents tend not to take pictures or keep a scrapbook of the early days if their child is premature or ill. But taking pictures even in the hospital and beginning the scrapbook then, helps you to focus on your little girl and the immediacy of her world.[1]

Try writing down what you feel in these early days at home. Whether you keep it as your personal diary or include it in your baby's scrapbook, writing will clarify your feelings and aid in your early adjustment. If you feel comfortable about it, you can share these writings with your wife. This will add to the feeling of closeness between the two of you.

Spend as much time as you can with your wife and child. Hold your baby, cuddle and explore her. Try doing specific tasks with her. Every task you perform with proficiency, no matter how small and seemingly unimportant, helps you feel good about yourself. And again, as your competence in caring for your infant increases, so will your confidence in yourself as a father.

Changing diapers is a case in point. Here is a simple task that is resisted with unflagging energy by many fathers. Yet once you give in and try it, you'll be amazed how good you'll feel about being able to do something that is a central part of your child's day-to-day care. I must confess I experienced my share of resistance. I had conveniently forgotten how to change diapers, although it was something that I had been taught at various stages of my career. I was chagrined when I realized that I needed to be taught once again with my own child.

You may not believe this, but once I started, I actually felt a sense of pride in changing my son's diapers. It was not that I enjoyed changing diapers, per se, particularly when he had had a bowel movement.

Rather, I wanted to be involved in what was happening to him. I realized that if I didn't change him, there was really not much I could do to participate in his care. As my ability to change him increased, I felt better about myself as a father.

If your wife is bottle feeding, take the opportunity to give your baby one or more of her feedings. Especially as you take the initiative in giving your baby her 10:00 P.M. or 2:00 A.M. bottle, you'll begin to think of yourself more as a part of the family. If your wife is breast feeding, bring the child in for one of her late-night or early-morning feedings. This is an activity that will force you to face the reality of her presence and give you an important role as a parent.[2]

Try bathing your child; bath time is a delightful opportunity for contact. And you'll feel good about having mastered what at first appeared to be a complicated job. Initially you may need help, but gradually you'll be able to do it on your own. Now you're becoming increasingly autonomous, deriving satisfaction from your developing skills and accomplishments with your new baby.

Taking some initiative in caring for your child may have dramatic repercussions for your marriage. New mothers often experience a feeling of being suffocated by the tremendous childcare demands on them. Your participation, even though you're doing it partly for yourself, gives her some relief from the feeling that she's alone in caring for the child. This early period can be an extremely dangerous time in the marriage, for you and your wife are both experiencing emotional strains. She may be feeling a letdown and some sadness and tearfulness, as well as anxiety. This is the state sometimes called the "postpartum blues." She may be overcritical and demanding of herself, uncertain of herself as a mother, and fearful of the change in her role.

Of course, you already know you're supposed to be especially kind, loving, and supportive of your wife during the early period after the birth. You know that this is a time when she feels vulnerable, that her body is undergoing major physiological transformations. But what is often overlooked is that you too feel vulnerable, anxious, and up in the air. So both of you need a good deal of support and understanding and will anticipate and expect this of each other. If this need is not met, each of you will feel hurt by the other's lack of response. This period is a challenge to the marriage. If it is well met, it can add a sense of richness and vitality, along with true intimate sharing between you. And as this occurs, you find yourself feeling closer to both your wife and your child and further along your journey of becoming, being, a father.

Receiving support may be easier said than done. You may be reluctant to talk about your struggles. You may feel withdrawn and unable to express your thoughts. Maybe you'd like to open up, but feel confused. Everything seems to be happening at once, all kinds of feelings, all kinds of demands. Everybody assumes that you should feel overjoyed and happy about being a father. And probably you do. Yet it is also normal for you to have feelings of fear, anxiety, dread, concerns about your ability to earn enough and support your family, sadness at what you may see as your lost freedom, and uncertainty about what it means to be a father. In the end, your efforts to express some of these feelings will be extremely significant.

Begin by sharing your fears and uncertainties with your wife. Be accepting of her own anxious or sad feelings. Try to keep the difficult issues aboveboard. Otherwise they tend to come out via anger, demands, and a critical attitude toward each other. The support of family and friends will also be of help to you in coping with this difficult phase.[3] And friends who have recently become fathers will provide a special ingredient. They affirm the universality of these experiences and can empathize with your struggles. Your laughter together will help you to transcend these early difficulties. The problems are still there, but somehow they'll seem less overwhelming. And don't be afraid to accept offers of help from your friends. You would want to help them if they were in need, so why not accept their help now. Be grateful that you have friends who care.

When friends and neighbors come to visit, follow these simple guidelines:

1.–Figure out what you and your wife can tolerate in the way of number of visitors. Otherwise you are likely to be overrun with people. Provide some structure and reason to the inevitable flurry of requests to visit. Your family needs some privacy.

2.–Keep in mind the sleeping schedule of the baby and your state of exhaustion. If the baby is asleep between seven and eleven in the evening, you may be delighted to see people at that time. But if your baby keeps you awake throughout the night, your exhaustion will make even these evening visits an unwanted burden. Perhaps limiting the frequency and/or duration of the visits will help.

3.–If you do have friends over, make it a simple occasion. Invite them for dessert and coffee rather than for dinner. You could ask them to pick up the dessert on the way over. The whole idea is to make this a pleasant, supportive contact with friends rather than a painful ordeal. You and your wife have enough to deal with without having to worry about being the perfect entertainers.

Grandparents too can be particularly supportive, and their presence can help you to cope with the stress and confusion of this period. The length of their visit or whether they should come at all depends on your feelings about having them. The central issue for you is whether you see the grandparents as people who will reach out and include you rather than shunting you aside. If your wife has strong feelings about wanting or not wanting the grandparents, then you may need to compromise.

Even if you have had a difficult relationship with your parents in the past, their visit can be a new beginning. For seeing our parents relate to our children allows for a healing of old wounds. It is as if our parents are giving to us through our child, and we experience pleasure and joy in this. Furthermore, the grandparents have an opportunity to relive some of the struggles of their own parenthood, which can be a significant event for them. And if they are truly motivated and concerned, they can be of immense help.[4]

The timing of the grandparents' visit should depend upon how involved you are able to be. If possible, take a week or more off from work in order to get to know the baby. Diving into the relationship early has several advantages. First, it helps you to feel like a participant from the beginning rather than an uninvolved bystander. Your immediate participation in the reality world of your child will help diminish your feeling of unreality or chaos and role confusion, as well as help you to focus on your child, to become engrossed in her. And of course your presence adds to your wife's sense of support.

If you can stay home and help with the baby for a week or more, then let the grandparents visit after that. Otherwise you may tend to take a backseat to the proficient and capable women. Some fathers, noting that a grandparent will be available at home, would be less likely to take off from work at all, feeling they would be unnecessary and even in the way. So urge the grandparents to wait before they come for any extended visits, unless for some reason you are absolutely unavailable. Their arrival as you return to work allows the period of support for your wife to continue unbroken.

Clearly, if the grandparents live nearby they will want to be with the baby as early as possible, and I think they should. But you can also let them know that during the first week, you and your wife would like to have an opportunity to get to know the baby together. Let them know that they are welcome, but also that your little family needs some time to be alone.

♦ Freedom: Lost and Found

Perhaps one of the most difficult struggles you will have to face following the birth is your fear of losing your freedom. You picture yourself as having to settle down, and maybe you're not ready. If you saw your own parents as having been trapped, inflexible, caught in a rut, never seeing the joy in life, you may fear that this will be your fate as well. You may find yourself asserting over and over to your friends your own battle cry: "It's never going to happen to me. It's true we've become parents, but our lives haven't changed."

It isn't so much change we fear but rather that we will lose ourselves, our individuality, our free spirit. If we knew that the change were positive, our fears would be considerably reduced. And the change can be very positive. Once you become aware that it is your freedom you are worried about, you can face it and deal with it. More than likely your wife has some of the same fears. If the two of you can discuss them together, you will both feel relieved, and you'll be less likely to feel the need to prove that you're a "free man."

It's true that your life is changing, but the entrance of the baby into your life allows you to discover new aspects within yourself. The joy of contact with your baby triggers your own intuitive, creative, and spontaneous side, the child within you. There is a sense of satisfaction and pride that comes with the realization "I'm a father, a father at last." Suddenly you begin to see your own life and your relationship with your parents in a new perspective. And finally there is a sense of meaning and fulfillment in knowing that you are connected with your child and your wife. You have embarked upon the path and are now setting upon your own journey. This is an exciting time. In many ways, you will be freer than you ever dreamed possible. You've discovered the ultimate freedom, that which comes from within.

•8•

The Perils of Responsibility

"His birth tied my working to the real world—providing for someone who depends upon me in a very real way. And rather than feeling a fear of that—'Oh my God, someone really depends on me'—I feel a sense of peace and calm in knowing where I have to go. I had a little freedom taken away, but it's good in the sense that it gives me a definite goal: to be an active father, to take care of my child, and in a society where most advantages are bought, to make enough money to buy him some of those advantages."

—Words of a first-time father three weeks following his child's birth.

Providing for your family is the activity that will preoccupy you in the months and years to come. There are tremendous pressures on you to produce and to "get ahead." If you haven't finished your education, or are on the lower rungs of the ladder in your field of endeavor, then the pressure is even greater. The problem is, how can you be a responsible father, provide food, clothing, and shelter, and still be available to your family? This is really the dilemma of our times. For in attempting to provide for your family, you are often removed from the home.

It is extremely important for a man to see himself as being able to provide. If he is not able to do so, he is likely to view himself as a failure. Even though his wife may work, he still feels that the ultimate financial responsibility rests on his shoulders.

Time and time again, fathers will talk of their close feelings for their infants yet spend little time with them, for they feel an incredible drive to make something of themselves now—before it is too late. The sense of aging and the pressures of responsibility create a time imperative. "It's now or never" is how this is often expressed.

Focusing on work also gives the father a role, a sense of direction that reduces the confusion and chaos of this early period. At least at work, things are more cut and dried, more predictable. As a father and provider there's nothing wrong with you putting a great deal of energy into your work. Not only can it furnish you with a much needed anchor, but the camaraderie of your colleagues may give you an emotional boost, especially if some of them are fathers and you can share your experiences with them.

My first days back at work made me feel that I was once again on solid ground. While the rest of my life seemed totally disorganized, I knew what was expected of me on my job. And I received a lot of acknowledgment from my colleagues about becoming a father. I enjoyed that, and I reveled in all the attention, the backslapping, and the kidding.

I had purchased two boxes of fine quality cigars imprinted with "It's a Boy," and I eagerly passed them out to the men I worked with. When one colleague said, "But I don't smoke," I urged him to take it anyway. Later, I realized that the process of passing out cigars to the other men was a symbolic act. It proclaimed to all the world: "I'm no longer a boy. I'm a father. Let's celebrate together." The cigar smoke among men was the sign that I had now entered a new phase in my life, that I had gone through a rite of passage.

I had entered the world of my father: the world of responsibility. A hint of this change could be seen in my sudden concern that my family have adequate protection in the event of my illness or death. Immediately after Jonathan's birth I called almost every insurance agent in town, attempting to get the best deal I could for medical and life insurance. I had never given any thought to life insurance, but now it was more than I who was involved, and I felt impelled to provide some sense of security for my family should something happen to me.

Something happen to me? Those words echoed in my ears. Such a thought would have been unheard of a short while ago. But now I was a man with responsibilities, and I had to consider my family. Responsibility is an inherent aspect of the way we fathers perceive our fatherhood. For example, a first-time father commented on this feeling even in the same breath as he described his relief:

> "The nine months when she was pregnant seemed to drag so long, now it seems like nothing. It's just over. I just feel all in. All that responsibility now!"

We worry about being able to provide for our family, regardless of our financial status. We concern ourselves with issues of security, regardless of how much security we have. You feel that everything rests on your shoulders. Previous to the birth, your wife may have been working. She may not resume work for several months or may decide to stay home during your child's early years. Perhaps you now see her as physically weak and vulnerable. And your baby daughter is so small and helpless that the weight of responsibility for her hits home like a ton of bricks. It seems awesome, and many fathers are overwhelmed by it.

Some fathers, fearing responsibility, run from it, leaving their families to fend for themselves without emotional or financial support. Others become so caught up with being responsible that they completely lose themselves in that role. They are good providers, but their family seldom sees them. There has to be a balance. The pressure to provide is real, but it can be coped with so that your work does not remove you from your family completely.

In the beginning, your wife may be pleased with your efforts to provide a better life for your family. For she too wants to create a home, a little nest secure from the onslaughts of the outside world. Encouraged by her, you feel an increased push to get ahead instead of just getting by. If your own family was plagued by financial hardships, you want to make sure that your child never has to go through that. This sentiment is seen in the words of a young father after the birth of his daughter:

> "I used to work a couple of days and make enough money and get by, and I could take a day off if I wanted to. Now, no, I don't want to do that! I feel completely different. I feel more obligated to my family, and what I want to do is work. I want to get ahead and give my family things that I never had. I can give my family a real nice life, make things easy.

Have the kids dress up nice in school. Give them the better things in life, why not? My wife wants it that way too."

The pressure on you can become even greater if your own life has been characterized by plenty, for you cannot accept anything less for your family. To do so is to feel that you have failed them. A first-time father put these demands into perspective as he talked about his baby daughter:

> "I wasn't worried that she was going to starve. I was just worried that she wasn't going to have what I had. I'd had a very good life. I always lived in the best neighborhoods, went to the finest schools, traveled all over the world, and basically had anything I wanted. That is something I was used to, and I felt that I would really like to have my child experience the same things. So I felt a certain amount of pressure. I felt that I had to achieve in order to obtain that kind of life for her."

If you're still feeling uncertain about where you fit into the family now, you tend to work even harder. But the more you work, the greater are your feelings of being isolated. And to compensate for that, you work harder—but this somehow results in your becoming even more isolated, from your wife as well as your child. What to do? It's as if everything is out of control. You gradually feel more and more detached from your new baby. You may even feel that you don't know your child at all. If you're going to hook up, you'll have to find a way to overcome this gulf between you. And sometimes it's not easy. For example, one woman described her husband's daily toil and the way it isolated him:

> "My husband works very hard, about eleven hours a day. He's only just now getting to know his three-and-a-half-year-old daughter. Last Sunday he went off with her for the first time in a long time. He hardly knows his baby son. He leaves while the baby is asleep and returns home when he's gone to sleep once again. He just feels so much his sense of responsibility."

It seems there are just not enough hours in the day, and you may feel you have no choice but to spend most of them working. If you don't provide for your family, no one else will. This struggle is reflected in the words of another first-time father:

> "When I'm working longer hours, I'm not home as often and I can't be with my child as much. But there's really nothing I can do about it. If I could stay home all day, keep up with my bills, and still keep my family going and be able to live a comfortable life, I would enjoy staying home with my child, spending all the time in the world with her. But in this society you can't; you've got to base your life around your ability to earn in the world and hope for the best."

There is a nobility in providing that is frequently ignored. Fathers who work and provide for their families are carrying out a valuable function. And in other cultures and other societies, this is enough.

The Siriono, a seminomadic Indian tribe in Bolivia, gives us an example of the importance of the father's providing role.[1] When the woman goes into labor, the father goes off hunting to provide meat for his family. The first animal that he kills will be the name given to the child, and the family name is also changed to this. If the infant is born while the father is out hunting, the cord cutting is delayed until he returns home, at which time the father cuts the cord. The birth is then followed by three days of highly patterned rituals and celebrations that involve the mother, father, and relatives. In this fashion the act of providing is not seen as separating or distancing the father from the family; rather, it is an integral part of the entire birth ritual.[2]

Many of the rituals common to agrarian and primitive cultures assure the father that his work is an important aspect of the family life. In these societies, however, the father's work does not remove him from the community for long periods of time as it often does in our culture. You probably work at such a distance from your home that it is not really a part of the community that you live in. In the agrarian communities of the past, where fathers worked long hours, the child could still be near his father, and his wife and infant might even visit him as he tilled the fields.[3]

So it is not so much the longer hours of labor as the separation of the workplace from the community that has resulted in the father's feeling increasingly isolated and excluded. Adding to this situation is the fact that your work schedule is not likely to have much built-in flexibility. Even when you're needed at home, such as when your child is ill, you probably can't take the day off to be with her.

The pursuit of responsibility is really a focusing on the protective function of fatherhood. In earlier cultures this included finding food, fighting off enemies, and gathering materials for a shelter. Nowadays this is largely expressed in your strong urge to take care of your family financially. Feelings of protectiveness begin during pregnancy and become stronger as the time of birth approaches. Some fathers express this by going out and purchasing a gun late in their wife's pregnancy. Some men sell their guns after the birth, while others hold on to their newly acquired weapons.[4]

This preoccupation with protecting your family also surfaces in your increasing concerns about the future, in your desire to plan ahead, to establish some feeling of control in your life. One father said:

> "It comes down to money; the responsibility that was my first concern was the financial responsibility. When it was just me and my wife, I was probably a little more content to just go along and make whatever changes I had to make when the time came. Now all of a sudden I find myself thinking about the future and planning for what I might have to do instead of waiting for it to happen. I don't want to be in a position where I'm scrambling to provide for my family. I want to have more control over it."

It is a sad statement of our times that the pursuit of responsibility, embarked upon for noble and unselfish reasons, can gradually lead to an erosion in the father's relationship with his wife and child, and even to a complete breakdown in the family. In less "advanced" cultures, and indeed even in the animal kingdom, the act of protection, in contrast to our Western society, often necessitates that the father be physically near his family. In certain fish, amphibians, and birds it is the male and not the female that protects and provides care for the young. The stickleback male fish builds a nest, attracts a female to spawn in it, then drives her out. He then fertilizes the eggs and cares for them by guarding and fanning them with a flow of current. When the young are hatched, he protects them from unforeseen dangers by carrying them in his mouth.[5]

The male sea horse appears to literally go through a pregnancy. The female deposits the eggs in the belly pouch of the male. This becomes enriched with blood vessels, like a superincubator. After thirty to forty-five days, the male appears to go through a process similar to labor, as the young, now sufficiently grown to face the sea on their own, are expelled from this breeding organ.[6]

Among the nonhuman primates, the protection the father affords often results in a close bond with the infant. For example, male Barbary macaques (Barbary apes) protect the young and carry them about on their backs as well as groom them. At times they develop such an intense bond with a specific infant that if it should die, they will carry its body about, sometimes for as long as two weeks.[7]

The birth of the newborn East African baboon in Kenya absorbs the attention of the entire troop, including the males. The most dominant males sit by the mother and walk beside her, intent upon protecting the new infant, which necessarily includes the infant's mother. Older males come and touch the infant and sometimes carry him for short periods. All of the adult males are sensitive to the distress calls of the infant and viciously attack any human who gets between the baby and the troop. Protection by adult males continues as the infant grows, and the relationship of infant to adult males is seen to be important at every stage of the baby's development.[8]

One researcher observed a mother baboon who was slow to respond to her baby's distress calls. A dominant male baboon began to watch over the infant and stay close to it. On several occasions he rescued the infant from near attack by threatening chimpanzees. When the infant died at three months, the dominant male continued his association with the mother only for as long as she carried the carcass.[9] It appeared that the adult male in protecting the infant had also bonded to him. It is also interesting that this male subsequently showed no further tendency to generalize his parental role to other infants in similar circumstances. He had bonded to that infant alone.

Among many animals, the protection the male provides results not only in bonding but also in the male's subsequently nurturing the infant. So it appears likely that in its instinctual basis, protection and nurturing are closely related to each other.

A human example of the power of protecting and its impact on bonding appeared on television in the story, "Father Figure." The father had deserted his family but returned for a two-month stay after his wife died. Toward the end of this visit, he rescued his eight-year-old son from drowning. This led to the father's having a feeling of closeness and a desire for increased contact. In effect, a bond occurred. The father became increasingly nurturing to the youngster and subsequently chose to reenter his life.

While this is only a television drama, the father's feelings are authentically drawn. The protection a father provides, when it causes increased contact, tends to lead to increased nurturing and bonding.

By nurturing I mean any activity that brings a parent into contact with his child. For example, holding your baby, cooing, singing, or talking to her, playing or dancing with her, or tickling her are all what I call *interactional nurturing* behaviors. And diapering, feeding, and bathing her are what I call *caretaking nurturing* behaviors.

As we became increasingly "civilized," the nurturing and protective functions began to become separated from one another. An indication of this separation was seen in the available literature. The father-child relationship was given scant attention. The father was viewed as a latecomer to the child's life who enters it only when the child begins to talk and become independent.[10] This literature made the assumption that women have deep psychological roots for motherliness but did not make similar assumptions about fatherliness. Fatherhood was seen as a social obligation rather than a state having biological roots and involving psychological satisfaction.[11] And the father's contribution was demeaned by designating as "mothering" any kind or solicitous care of an infant by a father.

Is it any wonder, then, that some men believe it is unmasculine to be nurturing? But this is simply not so. Nurturing is an intrinsic aspect of fatherly behavior and thus of being a man. It is neither borrowed from the mother nor an imitation of her behavior. Rather, it is unique in its own right and makes an important contribution to the child's development.[12] It is my view that the need to nurture is a natural masculine instinct that enriches both giver and receiver.[13]

I urge you to pay attention to your nurturing side as you provide security for your infant. Your closeness is important to her unfolding development. You and your wife balance each other, bringing different sets of behaviors into the relationship with the baby. This enriches the baby as well as yourselves.

The act of providing, particularly for new fathers, is often experienced as an act of love. The father sees his work as directly connected to his wife and child, and this gives it a new meaning. These thoughts are graphically captured by a new father who said:

> "I didn't want to take the traditional role, whether it was out of fear or just not wanting to become a wage slave—the old role of Dad going off to work, and us seeing him at about five until he falls exhausted into bed about nine.
>
> "Well, I was feeling this very strongly, especially toward the end of my wife's pregnancy. I was enjoying the pregnancy and getting far-out feelings. At the same time, I was working. There were all kinds of things I needed to do. I thought, if I'm going to get a teaching job, I have to finish my master's. The baby is going to come, my wife's not going to be working. I'm going to have to make all the money. How can I make money if I'm out at school doing my last semester work there? So I was feeling really trapped and had all kinds of misgivings about the future.
>
> "And then once he was born, that changed. Like him actually being here—it was like gosh, I've got this family, and it's wonderful, and don't you worry, I'll never let you down. I don't even know what I meant by letting him down. I was motivated to look at him and say, 'I'll never let you down,' and 'I'll take care of you.'
>
> "And then it became a very positive thing, that I would find a way. This crystallized something in me and made it seem a very natural thing, providing for him and my wife. And that was a strange, unexpected twist. It gave me a real necessity in life instead of an imagined one. It gave me something to live for."

In providing, you are showing how much you really care about your baby. If it is difficult to find time to make contact with her, let your wife know that you want more time with both of them. Your wife's support is crucial, for she can include you in the day-to-day happenings with your child. Maybe she can even bring the baby to visit you at work. This would give you the opportunity to cuddle and play with your baby when she is awake and alert, which gives each of you a chance to know the other.

Your wife does need to understand the pressures you must cope with. Then she can see that you are caught in a dilemma, and if you have not had much contact with the baby, this is something you might like to change. She needs to hear that you care, for she may also have felt isolated, overworked, and under pressure. There's no way for her to know that your focus on work is very much related to the new baby unless you tell her. If this is hard for you to express, perhaps these words of a first-time father may be of some help:

> "I am bound and determined to share as much time as I can with my baby, because I see that these times won't be around much longer. I want to give her the best quality time that I can. The first year is really important. It passes very quickly! I would hate to think three or four or five years from now that anything was more important than giving her the quality time that she needs right now!"

•9•

The Tyranny of Crying

Perhaps the most overwhelmingly stressful times that you will face as a parent are those when your child has continuous crying episodes. It makes you want to escape, to run and hide. You start asking yourself all kinds of questions: "Am I really cut out to be a parent? Have I made a terrible mistake?"

There is a universal chaos that is triggered by an infant's cry, and it is felt by mothers and fathers alike. Even the most experienced parents can be devastated by the shrill howl of a newborn baby, especially when the baby is unresponsive to their best efforts. You may find yourself becoming increasingly tense and irritable if you are frequently exposed to crying bouts.

Of course some babies cry much less than others. They have an easy temperament. They eat and sleep regularly and seem immediately responsive to your efforts to comfort them. If you and your wife have a baby like this, you'll probably remember the early months with pleasure. On the other hand, many babies eat and sleep less regularly and cry more frequently and for longer periods. During the first three to four months, many babies cry excessively regardless of their later temperamental styles. Some babies, particularly first babies, cry without letup for hours on end. Clearly this can be devastating to new parents.[1]

Despite the variety of responses, all babies cry at some point. We need to worry if they don't. For the baby's cry is a form of communication; it's the way he expresses his needs. And his cries inevitably cause an emotional response in you.

Dr. Peter Ostwald, while doing research on crying, often played recordings of babies' cries. He was frequently interrupted by some secretary in the building who had heard the cries, stopped her work, and come running to find out what was wrong with "the baby." Some made comments such as, "The poor thing must be hungry. Why don't you call its mother and make sure it gets fed." In one case a woman said, "Damn that brat! I wish the mother would come and get it out of here before I slash its throat." Dr. Ostwald concluded that there is something about a baby's cry that makes the sound easily heard and triggers a variety of responses, such as concern, protectiveness, and hostility.[2] And it is when your readiness to help your child cannot be translated into action, or when your attempts to soothe him meet with failure, that your frustration and tension become overwhelming.

Although babies do not understand spoken language, they intuitively perceive general feelings in the people around them. It is almost as if they feel through their skin. When you are with your child, he senses whether you're tense, angry, happy, or relaxed. A difficult situation with him can grow increasingly out of control simply because you feel out of control. Your child senses your anxiety and cries more loudly, which increases your feeling of being anxious and out of control. Nothing you do seems to relieve his distress. The continual crying reminds you that you cannot respond to his needs. Self-doubt and self-recrimination begin to heighten. You accuse yourself of being a bad parent. You see yourself as not meeting your own expectations about how you should perform.

It's painful to be reminded of your failures. You may become angry and frustrated with your child for his refusal to respond to you. Or you may simply withdraw from him. Whatever you do, you are likely to feel guilty. You feel guilty because you are angry at your baby; a tiny infant is not an acceptable object of anger. Or you feel guilty because you turn your anger inward on yourself rather than outward toward the baby. You may even feel sad and depressed. You may become irritated with your wife and find yourself suddenly enraged with her over a minor or imagined slight.

The cries of your child are like a plea for help. "Help me, Mommy, Daddy—do something." And they trigger vague memories of your past, of you as a child, of your own cries for help, for attention, nurturing, and support. That cry represents not only our newborn crying out to us but ourselves crying out to our own parents. To fail to relieve that cry is to leave the child within us in the lurch, to feel we have abandoned not only our baby but ourselves. This is a major reason the cries of the newborn are experienced so acutely.

I never truly appreciated the disorganizing impact of a baby's cry until I experienced it firsthand. Jonathan was about two weeks old, and Claudia and I had taken him on a small shopping expedition. I was relaxed and self-assured as I carried him in the baby carrier, which I had first used the day before. I felt very confident. After all, Jonathan was being the perfect baby—he was asleep.

But shortly after we arrived at the department store, Jonathan woke up and began to wail loudly. A whiff of a familiar odor caught my attention and I realized that he had had a bowel movement. We changed him there in the store, but this seemed only to make his cries more intense. It was a hot summer day. The sweat began to trickle down my brow, back, and armpits as I waited in a checkout line that seemed to last forever, with Jonathan shrieking louder and even more ferociously. I imagined that everybody in the store was looking at us, which increased my tension.

There was absolutely nothing we could do to comfort him. Claudia tried to breast-feed him when we finally got outside, but to no avail. The more he cried, the more tense and anxious I felt. Claudia and I began snapping at each other. We were both tight as coiled springs. The longer the crying went on, the more frazzled and disorganized I became. By the time we arrived home, after missing the right turnoff, I realized that I was having difficulty concentrating. I felt totally exhausted, as if I had been up for three nights in a row. With Jonathan still crying, Claudia and I sat down to eat lunch. I found myself becoming preoccupied with my own thoughts: "Oh my God, I'm never going to make it. Is this what being a father is like? Have I made a mistake? I feel like I've been through hell. My life is totally out of control!" I wanted to go off and hide, go to work—anything to get away from his crying. My ruminations were interrupted by Claudia saying, "Marty, I'm talking to you. I've been trying to talk to you for the last five minutes and you've just been eating pickles and staring off into space." I took a deep breath and tried to be more responsive, but I had no energy. I was like a racing car whose motor had suddenly burned up. I couldn't get rolling again. Shortly afterward, Claudia was able to get Jonathan to sleep. She said, "I guess he was just tired and needed his nap."

I was amazed that our son's crying could cause such intense chaos in me. However, as I reflected on some of my earlier experiences with parents, I remembered many situations that were similar to my own. When I was working as a pediatrician earlier in my career, young mothers would frequently ask for something to stop their colic-ridden babies from crying. When nothing relieved the infant's crying, they would invariably request tranquilizing medication for themselves. They described feeling as if they were going to explode, saying they could no longer withstand the crying.

You may ask yourself, Is this the same child we were talking about earlier, this adorable little bundle of joy who at birth caught us with his eyes, captured our imagination, and transported us into another world? Yes, this is that same child, and he can bring us to a moment of transcendence at one time, and plummet us headlong into the depths of misery at another.

♦ What You Can Do About Crying

If this seems like a bleak picture, don't give up; there is hope. Once you're able to get your child to respond, to quiet his screams, you'll feel a relief, a sense of pride and self-esteem, you never dreamed possible. To get to that point, however, you need to develop some basic confidence and competence with your child. And that means spending time with him, through thick and thin. It means, at times, hanging in there despite crying bouts and tolerating them long enough to learn how to cope with them. Once again, contact with your child is the final common pathway for resolving the problem. As you spend time with him you will begin to learn what works and what doesn't with his crying.

It helps to have some insight into the causes of crying in general. Of course, no amount of insight will alter your disappointment at your child's lack of response to you. But your awareness of his patterns and the knowledge that even the easiest of babies have their unresponsive periods will strengthen your resolve not to give up.

Patterns of relating are formed very early. You will notice this in your own young family as well as in the families of friends when they say something like, "Tommy always cried when I held him. I never could do anything right with him, so I gave up. I'm still not as close to him as I am to Maria, who has always responded to me." But it may be that the child who seemed unresponsive just needed perseverance and a little more effort on the part of the parent. And perhaps the parent needed an extra boost from a spouse, the support of family or friends, a nudge from the family doctor or the pediatrician, or a supportive therapist.

A number of things will help you in coping with your baby when he cries. First of all, you will gradually learn to recognize some of his needs by the sound of his cry, which will tell you whether he's just hungry or needs a diaper change, or if he's in pain. If he is not hungry or wet, make sure he isn't being poked by a sharp object such as a safety pin, that he doesn't have any open sores or a diaper rash, that he isn't too cold or too hot or in a draft. Babies sometimes cry excessively if they are becoming ill, so check him for a runny nose or feverish forehead. And remember that normal crying sometimes decreases or disappears as part of the lethargy of illness. If you suspect illness, consult your pediatrician. They also cry just because they are alone, and they respond well to being cuddled and talked to. Infants need human contact to grow and develop. Crying when they are lonesome brings them the loving contact they need. Newborn babies will not be spoilt by being picked up when they cry.[3]

In general, babies love music and rhythmic activity. Your infant may respond to your singing to him, to your dancing around the house with him. He'll like being bounced on your knees, and he may squeal with delight when you lift him up over your head or swing him up and down. You'll no doubt discover certain particular little tricks about soothing your baby. I discovered that when Jonathan became cranky he would gradually quiet down if I caressed his head. Even now, as a young boy, he still loves to have his head stroked.

Some babies seem to cry without rhyme or reason. Babies are called fretful if they cry easily and frequently but are usually responsive to efforts to quiet them. A baby who cries incessantly without apparent reason during the first three months and does not respond to efforts to soothe him is usually colicky. Colicky babies may cry without letup for two to four hours or longer, often toward the end of the day (although even noncolicky babies tend to cry most around the end of the day).

Some pediatricians think colic is caused by swallowing air. Others think it results from the infant's slowly developing nervous system, and there are those who blame it on the nervous state of first-time parents. Still others suggest that colic is a wastebasket term for something we do not understand. A variety of measures are recommended for the colicky baby. Unfortunately, most of them have uncertain effectiveness. However, if you do have a colicky baby, try whatever your pediatrician suggests. And you will be glad to know that this condition disappears by the time your child is three months old.[4]

Babies often cry when they are tired and need to sleep. If you stimulate them at such times, they will often cry longer and harder, and a vicious cycle sets in. If you just put the baby down and let him be for five to ten minutes, he'll probably drop off to sleep. However, sometimes he may have become so agitated that he is unable to sleep.

Whether your child's continued crying is the result of excessive fatigue, fretfulness, or colic, gentle, rhythmic movement in general will be of help. A rocking chair is a vaulable ally to the parent of a crying child. Or you can walk or rock him while holding him in different positions that he finds soothing. You can also take him for a walk in a baby carrier or backpack. The rhythmic motion of walking or rocking will often break through your infant's state of agitation so that he can calm down and fall asleep. (For a discussion of baby carriers, see Chapter 15, "Portapouch and Backpack." And for a discussion of holding positions that may soothe your baby, see Chapter 16, "Secret Weapons.")

The motion of an automobile can often be helpful. I remember an occasion when Jonathan had been crying shrilly and with increasing intensity. We thought he was tired, but we couldn't convince him to go to sleep. In desperation, after all else had failed Claudia and I, bleary eyed and exhausted by 11:00 P.M., loaded our shrieking son into the car and went for a drive. Within fifteen minutes he was sound asleep. Many parents have since shared with me the calming effect the car has on their babies.

There are other techniques you might want to try as well. For example, some babies are calmed by their bath, and this is something you could try doing for him. Also, babies seem to respond to low amplitude, droning types of noises, such as the hum of a hair dryer. An occasional puff of warm air from the dryer may also be soothing. Some respond to the rhythmic shaking of the washing machine.[5] Perhaps these various sounds are reminiscent of what the baby has experienced in utero with the surging movement of blood and the back-and forth motion of the cushion of amniotic fluid, all occurring against the backdrop of the mother's beating heart.

Some mothers report that the whistling of a teakettle stops their baby's crying. And others note that the relentless cries halt when the vacuum cleaner is turned on. Other babies respond to the vacuum cleaner as if it were some sort of wild animal and become more tearful and frightened. However, they may calm down if carried in an infant carrier while the vacuum cleaner is on. You might find that the motion of vacuuming while carrying your baby is calming to him, even if you're going back and forth over a clean and spotless floor. Your rhythmic movement and the continual hum of the vacuum may induce a state of slumber.

One mother told me that she would breathe in rhythm with her baby and then gradually slow down, and this would invariably calm and soothe him. That didn't work with Jonathan, however, because when I tried it with him I hyperventilated myself into a state of somnolence while he continued to cry.

Some of these techniques for reducing crying may even be effective in reducing tension later in life. For example, one woman, whose mother used to turn on the vacuum cleaner to quiet her as a baby, later discovered that her hair dryer produced a similar relaxing effect. She now uses this as a calming agent whenever she feels tense.[6] A friend of mine whose father was a musician was frequently calmed by music as a baby and young child. As a result, whenever he goes to a concert he finds himself, despite all efforts to resist, asleep within minutes.

One father I know plays the clarinet for his four-month-old son. The baby coos and smiles to the music, and moves his feet back and forth in rhythmic motions as long as his father plays notes in the lower register. However, he wrinkles up his face and cries at notes in the higher register.

You'll also find that various toys can catch your infant's attention and check his crying outbursts. If the toy makes noise when touched, this may be even more captivating. By three to four months your baby will be able to grab his rattle and shake it if you hand it to him slowly. And bright-colored objects passed in front of him will capture his attention, causing him to turn and look, often quieting him.

When toys are not available, you may be able to capture his attention with your voice. Simply say his name rhythmically several times then make cooing sounds and just keep talking to him. The excited inflection in your voice can frequently hold his attention.

One final technique. If your baby continues to shriek, you and your wife may feel as if you're in a torture chamber. There is no point in both of you enduring this for the entire time. Escapes need to be planned for. Parents are far better off if they relieve each other during stressful times. One parent should get out of the house for a while, perhaps to some friends or neighbors and do something enjoyable. That parent then returns fresh and full of energy, relieving the other and allowing him or her to do the same. This is part of a technique I call spelling, which is discussed in greater detail in Chapter 18.

There is no one hundred percent prescription for coping with your child's cries because every child is different and has his own way of responding. What works for one child may not work for yours, and you will have to learn to some degree by trial and error. But gradually, as you come to know your child's individual rhythms, you may find that his crying occurs at certain periods of the day. For example, babies often experience a surge of crying energy just about the time Daddy gets home from work. Knowing that you're not the cause of this may soothe your feelings of rejection.

There is another aspect of crying that can be particularly trying—the problem of crying in public. Parents often fear, "What if he starts crying in a crowd and people start looking at me and judging me?" The first time someone comes up to you and your shrieking infant and says "What's wrong with your baby?" it's as if a loud cymbal has sounded in your ears, confirming the worst of your fears. It's as if what was really said was, "What are you doing to make that baby cry?" You assume you have been found out, that everybody knows you're an incompetent parent. In fact, however, you are probably the only one who passes such a harsh judgment. You accuse yourself of being a bad parent and assume that others will do likewise. You feel guilty as accused—but the accusation comes from within.

Try not to let yourself get caught up in the fear of your child's crying in public. It will increasingly limit your freedom and flexibility with the baby. You fear he will cry if you take him out, so you don't. This makes you feel trapped and more anxious, so the baby tends to cry more and the cycle is perpetuated.

As you become increasingly experienced with your child, you will learn to read his behavior and gradually develop a repertoire of techniques you can use to soothe his crying. In addition, you can plan around the times of day he is likely to cry. Feeling more capable decreases your sense of helplessness and also reduces your tension and anxiety. This tends to have a calming effect on your baby, and you can be increasingly flexible with him. You can take him out and know that if he cries in public you'll be able to handle it.

Your ability to soothe your child's crying will enhance your relationship with him. There is something about going from the crying state of high excitation, agitation, and stress to the noncrying state of low excitation, calm, and tranquillity that seems to cement the bonding process. The more intense the crying, the greater the relief when it finally ceases. The calm after the storm is so pleasurable that it leads you to feel closer to your baby and increasingly engrossed in him, just as he tends to become increasingly bonded to that person who is meeting his needs at that moment.[7] As these events occur, you can respond to your baby's positive features rather than only to a raging mass of fury.

An unresponsive and crying baby is a major roadblock to bonding. But when you can face your infant's crying bouts without giving up, he will become increasingly responsive to your efforts. You will have made a positive start with him and will be off and running in terms of establishing a meaningful relationship.

·10·

Jealousy

> "My wife and I were really close. We would spend a lot of time together. We would walk together, hold each other, play cards, fish, or we would stay home and watch TV, lie on the couch together. Now whatever spare time we have together, the baby is there—and it's going to be that way for a long time. I couldn't accept that that's the way it has to be."
>
> —Words of a first-time father two months after his child's birth.

The single emotion that can be the most destructive and disruptive to your experience of fatherhood is jealousy. The potential for destruction, however, lies not in having the feelings but in burying them.

We all experience jealousy on some level or another at various times. To the degree that you can understand and bring these feelings into consciousness, you are less likely to be suddenly flooded with them and thus driven by them.

But why are you feeling jealous now—who are you jealous of? It may be difficult to admit to yourself that one person you are jealous of is your wife—of her relationship with the baby. You would like to feel close to the baby too. You wish you could be as capable and proficient with him as your wife is, that he would respond more to you. When you see how perfect your wife and child appear to be without you, you may wonder whether there is any room for you. You may wonder whether you're even needed. Feeling excluded by your wife, you are increasingly jealous of her and envious of her capability with the baby.

So you retreat into the background, angry, indifferent, and withdrawn

The feelings of jealousy toward your wife can be easily resolved if she reaches out to let you know that you are wanted and needed in the relationship. What may be more difficult to deal with is your jealousy of the baby. And you have good reason to be jealous. For the birth of the baby is affecting your home life in several important ways. For one, you and your wife have probably not resumed the level of physical intimacy you enjoyed prior to the pregnancy. Your level of lovemaking probably began to fall off during the last trimester of pregnancy and continued on this downhill course through the first six weeks after the birth. And even though your wife's physician has okayed the resumption of sexual intercourse, it may not always be easy to get on track again. There is less time for intimate moments, and your wife may be exhausted and temporarily less interested in lovemaking. When the two of you are interested, your baby's cries may disrupt you.[1, 2]

The increase of sexual tension sets the scene for trouble, especially if it is accompanied by a lack of communication. One father told me:

> "For the last six weeks of the pregnancy and for six weeks after the child was born, we weren't supposed to have any sex. That's three months. That's hard when you have that drive for sex and the doctor says no. It's best for her that you don't. But it creates problems too, especially for a man who loves his wife as much as I love mine. We stop having sex. We stop talking to each other. It all builds up and it's going to explode sooner or later."

There has been a basic change in your relationship. A new person has entered the scene, your wife is probably focusing most of her energy on the care of this little person. You may feel pushed out of the picture, as this father did:

> "Before you have a baby, it's usually just you and your wife. There's a lot of hugging and holding and kissing, and she's just really involved with you. After the birth, all of a sudden the baby is involved. It takes away from your space.

It's hard to have someone take away that space that you used to have."

Of course, if you've never really hooked up with your newborn and felt engrossed, you have an even harder row to hoe. For you are likely to experience your wife's attention to the baby as a rejection of you. Also, unless you've developed a relationship of your own with the infant, you'll be more likely to question your role in the family.

Perhaps it's hard to acknowledge your jealousy. You may try to downplay or deny those feelings. Even so, you have to admit that you don't have as much time with your wife as you did before. You may look forlornly back to the period when you had more time together as well as more time for yourself. This is reflected in the following words of a first-time father:

> "For me the jealousy is more a matter of time. All of a sudden a child comes along and it's a drain on time. I have to do more now to compensate for the fact that the baby is taking more of my wife's time. It gives me less time to do things I want to do. At times I get a little jealous of the fact that things have changed and they will be forever changed."

Your feelings of jealousy may erupt even when you feel most like a proud father, as you stand back in awe and fascination watching your wife breast-feed and care for your child. Perhaps you're not even aware of jealous feelings, for they are intermingled with love, pride, and acceptance. The only hint of jealousy may be a silent wish that you could be treated as well as your child. For example, when asked how it felt to watch his wife breast-feed their child, one father said:

> "It was really neat. It gave me a real warm feeling. When my baby was breast-feeding, it was like she was taking something of me and just really showing how much she loved it. Here is my baby, happy. And my wife is just really loving her to death. It's exciting to watch. Like why don't you do that to me!"

Your jealousy of the baby may also be related to your sense of lost freedom, your feeling that you can no longer come and go as you please. If you are a young father, these struggles will be greatly multiplied in intensity. You may feel trapped, and this triggers confusing feelings and increased tension, as seen in this father's statement:

> "My jealousy was coming out in all sorts of weird feelings. I would get mad and upset. I never felt this way before. You love your baby, but he's cramping your life-style. If you wanted to go to the movies, you couldn't go because the baby wasn't feeling good or something like that. You have to get used to that. But I wasn't used to that. I was just really getting wound up."

Perhaps you think you would be freer if only you and your wife could get out of the house, if you could be alone with your wife without the baby always intruding. You wish your wife could accept a baby-sitter once in a while, but she's still reluctant to leave the baby with others. A new father described his frustration in this situation by saying:

> "Yes, there is this certain jealousy factor between the father and his child. My wife gets so attached to the baby that she can't let her go, won't let her go. So then you start wondering how long is this going to go on? What the hell am I going to do? I wish that there was a reasonable amount of time when we could share our time together without our child."

Perhaps you have a hard time sharing these feelings with your wife, partly because your jealousy seems irrational or embarrassing, so you hold the feelings inside. This withholding tends to isolate you from your family. One new father said:

> "The baby had a lot of time with my wife and I didn't. She showed more love to him than she was showing to me. There was just my wife and the baby, and I wasn't involved. It sounds stupid. I was involved, but I was feeling that I

wasn't. It was because we weren't talking about the jealousy."

Often it's not the jealousy per se but the lack of awareness that leads to the irritability, hostility, and anger that can be so devastating to marital relationships. But the achievement of insight is easier said than done, as one new father realized:

> "It's hard for a man to accept his own feelings of jealousy. You are afraid to look at yourself and say, 'Hey, this is the reason why.' It's kind of hard to believe that some of these things can happen to you. If you don't want to face them, they happen."

And who is the cause of your jealousy and anger? Your baby. But since anger toward a helpless infant is not acceptable, the feelings may be redirected toward your wife. She is bigger and therefore a more appropriate target. This naturally causes your wife to feel that she's under attack. And she will probably defend herself by withdrawing so that she is removed from your critical eye. This vicious cycle is seen in the words of a new mother commenting on her husband:

> "He was feeling left out because I was giving the baby too much attention and not enough to him. At the time I was pretty upset with him, so I didn't really want to pay much attention to him. He was feeling rejected by me and I was feeling rejected by him."

If you were to say to your wife, "Hon, you know sometimes I actually feel jealous of the baby. I know it doesn't make any sense, but I still feel it," you would be moving that jealousy to a more positive level. Your ability to do this might encourage both of you to share your feelings. Your wife might say, "Well, you know that's interesting, because sometimes I feel jealous of your being able to go off to work while I'm all alone with the baby. And I do want you to spend time with her, but sometimes you act so tired or bored that I think you don't want to and that makes me upset and mad, because it's your baby too."

This honest exploration of feelings between you and your wife can make it easier for you to go beyond the jealousy. In fact, as the two of you really share your feelings, you are bonding anew. You are both getting feedback that you are valued individuals. The anger and mutual recrimination that occurred earlier was a trap that both of you had fallen into, and now you are digging yourselves out of it

I myself experienced jealousy toward my wife as well as our baby son. I became increasingly aware of these feelings as a result of an incident that occurred when Jonathan was about two weeks old.

I had just come home from work and, still wearing my suit, eagerly picked up a shrieking Jonathan to comfort him. But my efforts to soothe him were for naught; his howling continued. Moreover, as he continued to cry, I had this strange sensation of something warm running down my chest and legs. I looked just in time to see Jonathan leaking his bowel movement on my vest, shirt, and pants. My face dropped to the ground as I exclaimed, "Oh my God, I don't believe it!" I held Jonathan at arm's length as I carried him to his room and tried to change his diaper but was rewarded by even louder shrieks. "Now he won't even let me change his blasted diaper!" I said, totally exasperated. Claudia came to rescue me just as the situation was beginning to get out of hand. She thought that perhaps Jonathan was hungry, so she began nursing him. He immediately stopped crying and began cooing and gurgling, looking up at his mother happily. I knew Jonathan couldn't control his bowel movements and hadn't deposited his waste products on my suit intentionally. Nevertheless I felt rejected, hurt, and angry. I began to feel sorry for myself. I thought, "Claudia can respond to Jonathan in a positive way and he relates to her. When he's hungry, she nurses him. When I try to become involved by changing his diapers, he repays me by having a bowel movement on me. Is that fair?"

As I watched Jonathan nursing I was aware of many feelings. I felt jealous for several reasons. First I thought, "Gosh, what an incredible way for Claudia to get close to Jonathan. I'm envious. But there's no way I can experience that—I haven't got breasts! He must feel very close to the person that feeds him, and when he's hungry he's oblivious to me. He's only aware of his own needs and the pleasure that he gets from sucking and having his appetite satisfied."

In a way I felt jealous that Jonathan was getting all this attention. As I watched Claudia nurse him, I felt extraneous, unwanted, and removed from my family. His gurgling, sucking sounds of pleasure and my wife's peaceful smile confirmed in my mind that theirs was the perfect match, a blissful union of two lovers. The pride that I felt at other times when I watched the two of them had become transformed into a vague sense of discomfort, irritation, and anger. The relationship between my wife and our child seemed so perfect. How did I fit in? "Am I just the breadwinner who, having finished his job, then recedes into the background?" I was still struggling to find my own unique relationship to my wife and child.

My wife always seemed so attractive, so beautiful, as she sat down to nurse. I felt that I was competing with Jonathan for her attention, and on occasion this was combined with the feeling that I was a little boy. Out of nowhere would come the thought, "Hey, I want to nurse too. Move over, Jonathan."

Every marriage relationship has diverse aspects. You are a grown man, but at times when you feel weak and vulnerable, you may also feel like a little boy. There are probably times when your wife also feels vulnerable and wants to be held like a little girl, and you provided this support for her. But now your wife not only has less time for you but also less energy to respond when you feel like a little boy. She's already got a baby on her hands; she doesn't need two of them. This may be experienced as a great loss for you and, if it is not discussed, it can result in more anger toward the baby. This situation is captured in the following words of a first-time father:

> "Before our son was born there were times when I would come home and I would want to be the little boy. You know you have a parent-child relationship as well as a husband-wife relationship, and I don't mind admitting that at times I liked to be the little boy and just escape that way. My wife used to buy into that. I don't get that anymore."

Following the birth, these feelings of being like a little boy may be intensified by the childhood memories triggered by the birth. Along with this, you may increasingly begin to see your wife as a mother figure. In general, we tend to see our wives on many different levels. On the one hand she is the woman who is your lover, and on the other, she is the mother of your newborn baby. In the aftermath of the birth, when a woman's mothering role is emphasized, it is not surprising for you to see your wife primarily as a mother to the exclusion of her other aspects. Moreover, your decreased lovemaking enhances this focus. If you can't experience your wife as a lover, then the experience of her as a mother gains more energy and power. Intermittently you may even see her as your own mother.

All of these factors tend to increase the intensity of your little-boy feelings, and thus your sensitivity to a rival who, on some level, you fear will take your wife-mother away from you. If you had a sibling with whom you competed for your mother's attentions, your newborn may become that sibling for brief moments. In such a situation your feelings of jealousy may become so great that you are perplexed and completely overwhelmed.

But you do not see yourself only as a little boy. You are also a husband, a provider, a lover—and now a father. In that role you may feel closely identified and hooked up with your child. Sometimes in your closeness during the early months, you may feel as if that little baby is you and you are that little baby.

To see your baby as yourself?

To see your wife as your mother?

To feel like a little boy?

To be jealous of this child whom you have so eagerly awaited?

If these feelings appear irrational, it is only because we do not fully understand them. They are triggered by the emerging presence of the newborn, when feelings that are usually buried deep in the unconscious now come closer to the surface. To be made aware of the level of your jealousy is disconcerting. But the realization that these feelings are common to all fathers, whether or not they acknowledge it, may be of some help to you as a "becoming" father

Unlike the ambiguous guidelines outlined for fathers in our culture, many primitive cultures provide the father with strict rules of conduct.[3] In some cultures, the *couvade* is practiced. According to this custom, a father subjects himself to a number of regulations both before and after the birth of his baby. The most unusual is that he must remain in bed, frequently with his wife and baby, for up to thirty days after the birth.[3, 4] These regulations are thought to express a physical link between father and child in which the acts of the father are magically transferred to the offspring.[4] I wonder, however, if these regulations also protect the newborn from the feelings of jealousy and anger the father may experience following the dramatic change in his life situation. An example is the Kurtatchi people of the Pacific Islands. During the first three days after the birth the father is forbidden to lift anything heavy, do any work, or use a knife, ax, or other sharp instrument. If he does so, it is believed that the newborn will die. But on the fourth day he leaves the separate hut where he has secluded himself, sees the newborn for the first time, and gives him a special medicine that will make him strong. Anthropologists interpret this custom as a clear acknowledgment by the father of responsibility for his child.[5] But I believe that this ritual also symbolically acknowledges the father's potential anger and the harm he could cause the infant. At the same time it provides him with a positive way of averting this tragedy and even enhances the health of the child.

Unfortunately, in our rapidly changing industrial society we lack the rituals that help parents of more primitive cultures to cope with both the turmoil and joy of the parenting process. So fathers must struggle along on their own without much support or guidance. Being able to accept your negative feelings and share them with others will relieve you of some of the pressure. This is when it really helps to talk with other fathers, either alone or in a fathers' group. It is a great relief to learn that you're not alone in your struggles, that you're not the only one who has jealous feelings, and that these feelings can occur side by side with feelings of pride, love, and joy. A fathers' group can help you to get in touch with feelings you felt compelled to keep buried but can now experience without guilt. This kind of sharing with other fathers can slso encourage you to share the same feelings with your wife.

For information about these groups, consult your wife's doctor, her childbirth instructor, the local department of public health or community mental health center, or a regional YMCA that has classes or groups on parenting. Perhaps you can form a group by taking the initiative with the fathers who participated in your childbirth education class, having the instructor announce the formation of an informal group at the last class. Such a group could meet every two or three weeks following the births of the children and would be exceedingly valuable even if it met for just a few times.

Sometimes a father's feelings of jealousy and resentment become so overwhelming that he cannot find a way to deal with them. In such cases, further assistance should be sought. Perhaps you've tried to share your feelings with your wife, but both of you are too sensitive to make much headway. If there is no fathers' or couples' group available, it would be helpful to seek professional assistance. This could be a psychiatrist, psychologist, marriage and family counselor, social worker, nurse, pediatrician or family-practice physician—in other words, any professional who is interested in and knowledgable about bonding and the struggles of fathers. There is an increasing body of research and knowledge about this area. I have coined the word *parentology* to describe it and *parentologist* to describe individuals working in this field. So find a parentologist with whom you can develop a rapport to help you through your feelings.

You needn't feel embarrassed or ashamed of the difficulties you have during this early period of parenting. These are universal struggles that all of us experience, whether we acknowledge it or not. Your awareness and increasing ability to talk about your jealousy feelings will make it possible for you to transcend the problem and hook up with your little baby. For when you view his precious qualities, his smile, his lovely countenance, you will be able to see beyond your jealousy, which seems to diminish in importance. Your awareness will have gone a long way toward tearing down the jealous wall.

•11•

Humor: The Antidote to Taking Yourself Too Seriously

A sense of humor is absolutely essential in helping you to survive the early, trying days of parenthood. Taking yourself too seriously can be deadly. Being a parent is, of course, serious business, but cultivating a sense of humor will add richness and zest to this period.

I found that in those first months after Jonathan's birth I took myself too seriously. I was self-critical and demanding of myself, constantly looking to Jonathan for some affirmation of my importance. My search for a role, to feel a part of what was going on, was a dominant thrust in my life. As a result, I frequently overreacted to anything my son did that could be viewed as a rejection.

It's amazing how solemnly and with what consternation we meet some of our experiences as parents, and yet how hilarious they can seem later, upon reflection. When you look back on those early weeks with your baby, you may roar with laughter at yourself as you remember events that were definitely not funny at the time.

For me, giving Jonathan a bath was one of those times. When he was about a month old, Claudia encouraged me to try bathing him for the first time. I can assure you I would never have volunteered, for I had no confidence at all. I characterized myself as being clumsy with my hands even though I had actually handled many newborn babies as a pediatric intern. But this was different. I was being asked to hold my own baby, and suddenly I felt lost. I remembered one of the London fathers who had said to me, "I want to touch the baby, but I feel so clumsy because it's so small and me hands sort of swallow it.'' I felt a new surge of sympathy for him.

I tried to bolster my courage. I thought, ''Well, after all, if Claudia can give Jonathan a bath I ought to be able to do it too.'' I took a deep breath, thrust out my chest, pulled back my shoulders, and strutted forward, holding out my arms to receive my son. I moved with such stiffness and formality that you would have thought I was getting ready to perform a major surgical procedure rather than simply giving a baby a bath.

The first major obstacle I confronted was the coordinated use of two hands. My goal was to hold Jonathan securely with one hand to keep him from slipping into the water and to suds and rinse his body with the other hand, all the while keeping an agreeable chatter going with him. In my novice state this seemed terribly difficult and complicated. I found that whenever I was successful in moving my hands with some sort of synchronous activity, my mouth closed. The movement of one seemed to foreclose the activity of the other. Finally Claudia, who was watching intently, could no longer contain herself. ''Honey,'' she said, ''try to talk to him while you're bathing him.'' I tried very hard, and as much for my own benefit as for Jonathan's. ''Come on, Jonathan,'' I said, ''this isn't going to hurt—your daddy wants to give you a bath. Jonathan, it's okay. You don't have to scream. Give me a chance.''

But when I opened my mouth my left arm stopped moving, and I couldn't figure out how to lower Jonathan into the water and rinse off the soap with only one hand. Washing his hair and trying to keep the suds from drifting into his eyes seemed even more complicated. And although the baby shampoo was not supposed to burn, he seemed to find it irritating and struggled and cried even more.

The Red Cross and various parent manuals write about the technique of bathing a baby, but frankly it all sounds much easier than it really is. When you get right down to it, it's an amazing feat. After all, you have an incredible responsibility on your hands. And all the while I'm thinking, ''My God, he's slippery. What if he should fall?'' This thought seemed to inhibit the motion of my arms even more.

Meanwhile my wife, who was peering over my shoulder, was wondering about the apparent paralysis of one arm. ''Hon, why aren't you using your other hand?'' she asked, apparently not understanding that when my mouth moved my arms stopped.

Throughout the bath, Jonathan cried at an increasingly intensive pitch. Of course, he also wailed when Claudia bathed him, but now I imagined he was saying, "Get away. I don't want a bath from you. I want Mommy to take care of me." Claudia always seemed so comfortable, skilled, and relaxed as she talked and cooed to him during his bath. My own efforts paled in comparison. I experienced a new-found respect for her child-bathing talents, and at the same time I felt as if a massive stone had been placed on my back, immobilizing me. My face became flushed. Sweat began to soak through my shirt. I felt like hiding and fading into the woodwork. How could bathing one little baby have so much power over me?

All this seems hilarious to me now, remembering how embarrassed and frustrated I felt, and how tied into knots I was by my own inexperience and the desire to be important to my baby. I have since found, and I expect you will too, that when I could eventually lower my defenses and share some of these seemingly "crazy" and embarrassing episodes with other parents, it triggered similar uproarious stories from them. I hope telling you some of my stories now will help you to gain perspective and see the humor in your own situations.

When Jonathan was three and a half weeks old, Claudia became concerned about his circumcision. It seemed to have been ineffective, and she wanted to get my "expert" psychiatric opinion. As I bent down to take a good look at Jonathan's penis, I got a direct hit of urine right in the eye. Thank God I was wearing my glasses. Only a few drops splashed into my eyeball, but this was enough. Yelping in pain, I dropped Jonathan's member, and ran to the bathroom to rinse out my eyeball, all the while muttering under my breath.

Actually, I think I was experiencing more of a blow to my ego than pain to my eyeball, because I felt embarrassed and humilated. And I felt, unreasonably, that Jonathan had set out to urinate on me with some sort of conscious intent. Newborns have an incredible ability to bring us down to earth, especially when we try to cloak ourselves in some kind of role as an expert. They force us to deal with them right now, in the present.

Meanwhile, with my first cry of dismay I had caught a glimpse of my wife, who was now overcome by laughter. This lent more than a morsel of support to the nagging suspicion that perhaps she had known all along it was time for Jonathan to relieve his bladder. "Hon, you looked so funny," she said. "It's not so funny," I grumbled.

Nevertheless I broke into a smile and at last, in spite of my efforts to keep a straight face, exploded into guffaws. Afterward, whenever I had to check Jonathan's circumcision or change his diaper, I automatically covered his genitals with a diaper. I did this with such religious zeal that you would have thought I was a priest consecrating a hallowed relic of worship.

Claudia had continued to nurse during this early period, but by the time Jonathan was a month old, the pediatrician urged her to start giving him a supplemental bottle. She felt somewhat dejected about this. She enjoyed breast-feeding so much that she was reluctant to lose any part of this beautiful experience. As a result, she put off following the doctor's recommendation for about a week. Eventually, however, with a stiff upper lip she encouraged me to give Jonathan his first bottle. To say that I was eager would be an understatement. I was like a race horse chomping at the bit to have the gate opened so I could be the first one on the track.

I had on numerous occasions witnessed the immense power of my wife's breasts. Apart from being more ample than they used to be, I was astounded by the almost magical control they exerted over Jonathan. Like the benevolent wand of a sorcerer, they suddenly cast a beneficent spell. While he suckled, his thrashing about, screams, and cries would suddenly be replaced by gurgling, smacking sounds of pleasure. His entire body relaxed, and he would give me a glimpse of a fleeting smile as he drifted off into slumber. As Jonathan suckled, Claudia would herself undergo a transformation, smiling blissfully while she embraced and stroked him tenderly as if she were caught up in the power of her own enchantment.

I had assumed that the magical wizardry that Claudia exerted over Jonathan resided in the food itself. I ought to be able to duplicate this magic, I reasoned, with a concocted brew of my own preparation (namely, cow's milk), served in a special vessel with a rubber sucking device on the end (a baby bottle). This was a little bit like thinking that taking on the habit of a religious man made you a priest. But so enthusiastically was I caught up in the notion that I was now going to become a wizard in my own right that I failed to consider the possibility of failure.

I tried to find a leisurely position while feeding Jonathan. Our sofa seemed like a good idea, but this was somewhat deceptive, for like quicksand, it had a tendency to cave in as you sat back on it. The soft cusions made me feel pleasantly enveloped at first, until I noticed that I was gradually disappearing into the yawning gulf between them.

Claudia, actively coaching me, said, "Now get into a comfortable position and put your left hand around his back so you've got him in the crook of your arm." I held Jonathan in both arms, trying to get into a comfortable position using only my legs. I fidgeted about, attempting to find a pleasant position while pushing my legs against the floor for leverage. But as I turned, the weight of my behind drove me deeper into the sofa's crevices. As this battle with the couch raged on, I realized that in my nervous anticipation of feeding my son, I had embraced and intertwined my arms around him and nearly lost track of which was my left and right side.

Claudia had been silently watching me work myself deeper into the couch. She finally came to my rescue and said laughingly, "Hon, you don't look very comfortable at all. Use the armrest of the couch for support." And she demonstrated the position for me. At last, following my wife's counsel, I settled into a more relaxed posture, using the armrest to keep from sinking into oblivion.

This was supposed to be the big moment. Anticipating the pleasure of our skin-to-skin contact, I took off my shirt and eagerly thrust the bottle's nipple into Jonathan's mouth, fully expecting to hear the same sounds of satisfaction my wife's breasts elicited. Sadly, this was not the case. Jonathan apparently sensed the difference because his response more closely resembled anger than pleasure. He thrashed about, jerking his body in different directions as he tried to clasp his mouth around the nipple. His vigorous activity succeeded only in knocking it from his mouth, at which point he began to cry, upset that he had lost his supply of food and seemingly angry with me for being the cause of his problems. When he succeeded in finding the nipple his howls of displeasure abated for a minute or two until he dislodged it once again. This resulted in more shrieks, and it was during these ear-shattering blasts that the thought flashed through my mind that perhaps changing diapers wasn't so bad after all. At least, I reasoned, there was no deluding yourself. You knew exactly what you were in for.

After some thirty minutes of continuous struggle, I was relieved to find that Jonathan had finished his bottle. "I did it. That wasn't so bad," I said to myself as if I had just been through some sort of rite of initiation. That was the way I used to feel after I had been up all night three days in a row studying for my final exams. "How do you feel?" my friends would ask after finals. Eyes bloodshot, head aching, face unshaved, teeth unbrushed, clothes disheveled and unchanged, and body reeking from the sweat of the past three days, I would answer with a broad grin, "Oh, I feel great. Boy, am I glad it's over. You know, it wasn't that bad after all."

With the feeding completed, I assumed anything else would be a bed or roses. So when Claudia suggested that I burp Jonathan, I did so confidently if not enthusiastically. I patted his back once, nothing happened; twice, nothing happened. On the third pat . . . Eureka, results! And how! With a loud, deep, and prolonged belch, Jonathan spit up all that I had struggled so vigorously to get down him.

My look of utter shock and dismay must have caught my wife's attention because out of the corner of my eye I noticed that she was undergoing an enormous struggle of her own. Holding her fist against her mouth like a gag, she tried to stem the flow of laughter that threatened to overwhelm her. Jonathan, meanwhile, looking as delighted as I have ever seen him, had suddenly brightened and seemed quite pleased that he had been so successful in removing that giant air bubble. By now, Claudia was unable to contain herself and was almost hysterical with laughter. I stood stunned and frozen in place, partially digested milk dripping down my bare chest and back. The more I frowned, the more Claudia laughed, and the happier Jonathan seemed to become. I felt abused, irritated, and annoyed. I gave Jonathan back to Claudia and headed for the shower, grumbling, "First he craps on me, then he pees on me, and now he throws up on me. Is that any way to treat a father?" I was like the pitcher who never could throw a complete game. Shoulders slumped and feeling dejected, I was ejected from the game by my son, Jonathan, who always seemed to be sending me to the showers. I felt like a guy who had just had a pie thrown into his face, and I didn't find it funny—that is, not until I'd had time to reflect on it several days later.

It was as I looked back on these experiences and remembered how serious I was that I saw how funny they really were. And I came to realize that a sense of humor and the ability to laugh at ourselves is one of the most important attributes we can cultivate as parents. What more loving way to communicate than to laugh together, retelling stories of early struggles, laughing so hard that tears flow down your faces. It is truly wonderful for children to see their parents this way.

The situations that once caused frustration and anger now become a source of pleasure as you share them with each other, with your children as they grow older, and with other couples.

A child really forces you to get in touch with your sense of humor. You have to, to keep from drowning in your own serious expectations of yourself and the demands others have made on you. Children trigger so many "shoulds" and "oughts," in all of us. You think you should raise your child in this way or that to be a "good" parent, for fear that otherwise your friends and neighbors may say things like, "You did *what* with your child?" "You took him outside before he was six weeks old?" "You let him cry *how* long?" "You gave your child *what?*" and so on. In this sense, the birth of your child is an entrée into the powerful world of society's proscriptions and demands. But by getting in touch with your sense of humor you can moderate these pressures. It's as if you can dive underneath a giant wave, just before it breaks on shore, and in this fashion mute its impact.

Similarly, laughter allows you to break out of the trap of your own rigid demands and expectations. It allows you to see your own inflexibility and thus offers a way out. In so doing, without realizing it, you transcend your adult focus on intellectualizing and logic, and enter the spontaneous and intuitive world of the child. Your laughter allows you to make a deeper connection with your child, to relate to him in the real world.

The key to achieving this happy state is: Don't take yourself too seriously. To be rigidly serious is like gulping down a deadly potion. It dulls your mind and diminishes the sights and sounds of events occurring around you. It forces you to make a wry face when you think of an earlier painful time and prevents you from seeing the humor inherent in it.

If you can take a small step back, enough to allow yourself to laugh, you will open up a new side of yourself. And by your spontaneous guffaws you will generate a newfound source of energy, giving your life enhanced meaning and vitality. To be able to laugh is to free yourself up, to move on the wings of the spirit, to truly reach inside and touch the joys of fathering, of parenting, and inevitably of life itself.

•12•

Recharging Your Parenting Battery

Despite the feelings of love you and your wife have for your little daughter, there will be occasions when the two of you may feel as if you have no more energy to respond to her. You feel drained, exhausted. The two of you can put so much effort into your child and get so involved in her day-to-day care that your parenting batteries begin to run down. And you need to have ongoing ways of recharging them.

• Breathing Time

The newborn baby generates such an incredible amount of power and energy that it is not surprising that parents find themselves totally focused on their baby. But if that focus excludes everything else, you can begin to feel cut off and trapped. You feel drawn in by a magnetic field, yet you also feel the need to escape.

The answer to this problem is *breathing time.* You need some time away from the baby, time to focus on your relationship with your wife and to take care of your individual needs. The best way to get some breathing time is to get out of the house, for whenever your infant is present she will dominate. She is so adorable, so cute, that she overrules all other considerations. Your wife will probably not feel comfortable about leaving the baby with a sitter for the first few months, and this is understandable. But if the baby's grandparents are in the area, the situation may be simplified. You know she is with people who really love and care about her. But even without grandparents, the two of you still have other resources. You and your wife could agree to split child care with a friend, with you caring for their child one night while they care for yours on another. Or perhaps you know an older nurturing woman whom you both feel good about. Or you could get a neighbor to watch the baby while you take a walk around the block together if you don't feel comfortable about straying farther afield.

Where you spend your time together is less important that how you spend it. Basically, it's important that you allow yourselves a relaxed way of being together, an opportunity to talk and have fun. You and your wife could go out to dinner, take a long walk, go for a drive or picnic, visit a museum or art gallery, see friends, or even go to a party. If you enjoy sports, depending on your wife's level of energy, you could swim, play tennis, or go to a football or basketball game. And an occasional film or play will give you an added sense of freedom, for you are now doing something that perhaps you thought would be off limits to you once you became a parent.

It's a good idea, however, not to go to a party, film, or spectator sport unless you know you're also going to have some time to be alone together. If you have only a short period of time away from the baby, choose an activity that will allow the two of you to talk and hook up with each other. You need time as a couple to share your uncertainties, desires, and intimate feelings. Although you are now parents, you are still husband and wife. And you need nurturing as a couple. Otherwise, you will increasingly come to feel like strangers in the same house.

If for some reason you and your wife cannot or are unwilling to leave the baby even for a brief period, you can still have some breathing time together. There will be more obstacles in the way, but they are not insurmountable.

Try to set up a kind of sanctuary in your own home, a safe and secure space that removes you from the rest of the world for a while. This depends greatly on your infant's sleep schedule. Within a couple of weeks you'll have a pretty good idea of what that is, although you may have to adjust to gradual changes. Plan to spend your time together during those sleep times. To assure a feeling of peacefulness, do the following:

1. Put distracting things aside. This means the newspaper, magazines, mail, and bills.
2. Take the phone off the hook or unplug it (an hour or two won't

hurt). If you were out of the house, it wouldn't get answered. So pretend you're out of the house.

3. Let your friends and family know when you will not be available. Most of them will respect your need for privacy. It's your right—you don't have to apologize for it.

You may not be able to take this time alone together every day, but you will need at least several hours a week to benefit from it. Plan a regular time that you can look forward to. Up to an hour or two a day will do wonders for your marriage as well as giving you renewed energy and resourcefulness in your parenting roles.

The tension of these early months, as we have said, comes from a number of sources: from your wife's increased fatigue after the birth, from the uncertainty both of you feel in your new roles as mother and father, and from your own heightened sense of economic responsibility. It is also closely related to how much your baby cries, to how soon she begins sleeping through the night, and to the degree of support you and your wife have from other sources. In response to these tensions you and your wife can easily get on different tracks, you focusing on your work and she giving all of her attention to the baby. This is a natural tendency for most new parents.

This sense of being on different tracks is further exaggerated by the decreased frequency of lovemaking that inevitably follows the birth. The pregnancy may have altered your normal pattern of sexual intimacy, and the baby's arrival may further disrupt things.[1] During the pregnancy, of course, the two of you had a goal, a healthy baby. Now that the baby is here and your wife is returning to her nonpregnant form, you may find it harder to continue to delay sexual gratification. Some men are not convinced that there are medical reasons for postponing their needs. They feel unable to wait the customary six weeks and try to talk their wives into resuming sexual relations earlier. They may beg, plead, and cajole, trying to convince her that a few weeks more or less is not going to do any harm.

If the wife is also eager to get started she probably won't blame her husband for encouraging her to violate her physician's orders. On the other hand, his insistence on gratifying his own needs without regard for her welfare may result in her becoming annoyed with him. She may have had an episiotomy and worry that intercourse so soon will be painful. She may fear that something could be torn inside and that she would suffer serious damage. A woman may be completely healed but still be fearful. And perhaps she senses that her fears are unfounded and yet cannot discuss them. If she finally talks about her fears and her husband ridicules them rather than responding with understanding, she'll probably respond with anger and resentment. Both husband and wife then begin to berate each other for a lack of caring and consideration. Thus the stage can be set for anger, isolation, and mutual recrimination. For these reasons you and your wife should have a discussion with her physician regarding sexual relations. Ask questions; find out the physical realities of the situation. Your physician may explain that one of the problems that couples have at this time is a feeling of isolation from one another. And even if intercourse is not immediately resumed, couples need to be in touch with one another, to be able to embrace and express tenderness to one another. Furthermore, he may explain that mutual caressing is another way for both of you to meet your emotional and physical needs at this time.[2]

Often the six-week date is an arbitrary, physician-imposed deadline. Given feedback from you and your wife, your physician may alter it. And very importantly, you will have taken part in a major discussion that affects you.

Masters and Johnson report that many women report a decreased desire for lovemaking during the first three to four months after the birth.[3] If this is true of your wife, it will probably be a disappointment, for you have waited your six weeks or longer, and it doesn't seem fair. Your wife may be reluctant to touch you or kiss you for fear you will get the wrong idea. So she withdraws physically. In the tense atmosphere following the birth, rebuffs, especially sexual rebuffs, are taken much more personally.

On the other hand, perhaps you too have less interest in sexual relations now. Sometimes it takes time to integrate your images of wife and mother. And your continuing abstinence from sexual relations tends to beget continued abstinence. In this circumstance, the six-week deadline can be seen as an expectation, perhaps even a demand to perform, for the both of you!

Even when you are back on the lovemaking track again, the baby is always a potential interruption in one way or another. If your wife is breast-feeding, the baby's cry will often result in a reflex release of milk, which is a disruptive sensation for both of you. And even if you've both agreed that one of you should respond to the baby the mo-

intimacy. If you've decided the baby can wait five or ten minutes longer, you may find that a "let's get this over with" attitude prevails. But beyond that, marital problems increase if there is a lack of consensus about how soon to respond to the baby. It is to escape such dilemmas that some couples leave their newborn at the home of friends or in-laws or escape to the solitude of a motel.

The sheer physical demands of taking care of a new baby can also have an impact on a couple's sexual relationship. One couple were kept constantly preoccupied with their three-month-old, who was fretful from 5:00 P.M. to midnight. By that time sex was no longer of interest to them. The husband said:

> "By midnight I was so exhausted I didn't even have time to think about sex. I just plopped into bed and immediately fell asleep."

Some couples' intimacy is stifled because the baby sleeps in the same room with them. They fear that the sights and sounds of their lovemaking might somehow harm their infant's emotional development. They may attempt to schedule their intimate time, resulting in a great loss of spontaneity.

Intimate time in general, not only in relation to sex, is at a premium during the early months after the birth. Breathing time helps regain some of that time for you, time when you don't feel rushed, time to make love, time to laugh and joke together, and time to show that you value each other. Perhaps now, more than in any other period, your wife needs you to be caring and loving, but not only as a prelude to sexual relations. There may be times when she only wants you to hug and hold her, and it will help if she can tell you this. You may discover that you also want and need to be held. Touching each other increases your feeling of closeness and intimacy. You are letting each other know, "I'm not making any demands on you; I care about you unconditionally."

Whether you use your breathing time for physical intimacy or for just being together, it will vitalize your marriage. You will find additional energy to respond to your baby with greater pleasure and flexibility. While paying attention to your marriage, you've recharged your parenting battery. Your relationship as a father to your child now occurs against the background of your positive role as a husband to your wife. It is a part of the whole.[4]

♦ Meeting with Other Parents

Support and reinforcement from other new parents will also help keep your battery recharged. New parents today face different kinds of stresses than were experienced several decades ago. No longer can a couple take it for granted that people will value them simply for having become parents. Fathers face the difficult task of coping with occupational demands while attempting to enter their child's life; and women face the complex task of meeting their child's needs while making the decision about whether to stay home with their baby and if so for how long, before they face the next difficult question of whether to resume their own careers. Add to this your own high expectations of yourselves as parents, and you have a recipe for uncertainty and anxiety.

To deal with these feelings, you and your wife need to have contact with other parents. You will find that each couple has something to contribute to the other that helps relieve some of the feelings of stress overload. In a sense, by sharing problems and joys you become positive culture carriers for each other, each couple contributing the unique aspects of their own experience. This positive and loving support helps to sustain emotional growth during your development as mothers and fathers.

In socializing with other parents, you will have some choice as to whether or not you will bring your baby. Our preference was to socialize without Jonathan about once a week. However, we took him along at other times and this also worked out well. So if you and your wife feel uncomfortable about leaving your baby, take him along. You'll be amazed how just getting out of the house, even with the baby, can give you a renewed sense of freedom. This is because new parents, particularly young parents, frequently overreact to the novelty of their new role and assume it with overseriousness. They tend to be too hard on themselves and allow themselves little flexibility. But by building early flexibility into your role as a parent, you increase the rewards and the sense of pleasure associated with parenting.

My first realization of the importance of contact with other parents occurred when I attended Claudia's childbirth classes with her. There was a great deal of reassurance in discovering that other men were experiencing the same feelings I had. The commonality of an experience serves as a bond between people. There is a feeling of closeness and support that explains to a large degree the power of sharing within a group. And I am talking about groups for fathers alone, mothers alone, or fathers and mothers together. All of these groups have their valid points.

During Claudia's pregnancy we became acquainted with another couple named Darrell and Sharon. Sharon was due one month before Claudia. The two women shared ideas, thoughts, and reflections during the pregnancy and thus drew closer. We two expectant fathers also began to share our concerns and feelings about becoming fathers. I found this particularly helpful, especially as my anxiety level rose as Claudia's due date approached. Our friendship continued after the birth of our children, both boys, and I found our contact helpful and supportive in my evolving role as a father. Perhaps the most meaningful thing for me was when we shared our anxieties and concerns and were able to laugh together in the face of our early parenting struggles.

When Jonathan was about six weeks old, we two couples went out to dinner, leaving our newborns at home in the care of others for the first time. I remember feeling it was hard to believe that Jonathan wasn't with us. It was almost as if I felt naked without him. Our two boys seemed to be the sole topic of conversation during dinner. The evening was highly charged, and I realized that our expression of feelings about our children defused an incredible amount of anxiety the first night away from them.

New parents become anxious about so many things—about their performance, about their inability to get their child to respond, about their child's health and well-being. Darrell, for example, shared his experience of his son's first night at home, and we all chuckled as we identified with his struggles. He said:

> "The first night the baby was home from the hospital, we put him in our room. Sharon slept fine, but I was up all night. He kept making all kinds of noises. He would cough or sound like he was choking, and I would leap out of bed and stand beside his bassinet thinking he was having trouble

> breathing. After a couple of nights like this I decided I wasn't going to survive unless we put him in his own room. I wasn't getting any sleep. Now I can hear him well enough when he cries, but not so well that I leap out of bed with the slightest cough."

And I in turn told them about one of the first times I had taken Jonathan in the car alone, when he was two weeks old:

> "I was feeling pretty proud of myself because earlier that morning I had carried Jonathan in the baby carrier. I felt pretty cocky, really like a good father. I was driving around with him asleep in the car bed, still wearing his baby sling. Well, all of a sudden I got worried by the silence—no noise. Silence can be deafening. I suddenly felt scared. I glanced at the backseat and I couldn't see his head. I slammed on the brakes and pulled Jonathan out of the car bed. He had kind of slipped back into his baby sling. I was terrified that he had suffocated. As I picked him up I thought, 'Oh God, please Jonathan, breathe.' You can imagine how fast my heart was beating. Jostling him around woke him up, and he let out a loud shriek. You can't believe how happy I was to hear him cry! But I sure felt like a lousy father for not taking him out of that baby carrier."

Laughing at my anxiety helped take away some of the guilt I felt. It wasn't a funny situation, but I could now put it into proper perspective. In meeting with other parents, perhaps you can share how the focus of your life has changed. You may realize that the main thing that has changed is your concept of yourself. For you now view yourself in a different light. You're a parent and you feel a greater responsibility in your new role, not only about day-to-day practical matters but about your child's future and your value as a father. You will find that many of your concerns and questions are universal themes shared by all fathers.

"What kind of a father will I really be? How will what I do affect my child? What kind of a child will I have? What kind of a person will she become? Will she be intelligent? Will she be a professional, have a family of her own, or be a vagabond? Will she appreciate and value life? Will I be able to guide her effectively? Will she feel that I am a good father? Will I be able to help her find what she wants to do with her life? Will she be a good and decent human being? How will I impart to her the values I feel are important? How can I give her a thirst for knowledge, an appreciation of her fellow human beings, a joy in living, an appreciation of the wonder and beauty of nature?" Many of these issues seem so far away, yet they may also be of great concern for you now. As these kinds of questions come to mind you will realize that you feel many different types of responsibilities for your child, not only financial responsibility but responsibility for her mental and emotional development—and they are all related.

It is in a group that you will find you can voice these questions and express your hopes as a parent. The other parents provide a key ingredient, allowing you to discover new aspects of yourself as well as helping you to cope. The presence of other parents is a powerful battery recharger. It gives you a renewed determination and increased energy to push ahead with what is at times the difficult yet rewarding process of being a new and involved father.

·13·

Sharing: "Twinkle, Twinkle, Little Star"

Seeing your child's smile for the first time is an overwhelming event. It can knock you right off your feet. If you've had trouble hooking up with your child, or if your work has distanced you from him, his first smiles will reorient you.

Researchers in child development say that the infant's smile is a powerful stimulus with a biological basis that results in the attachment of mother and infant.[1] I'm quite sure the smile has a similar effect on the father.[2] Many fathers have described this event to me, and I experienced it myself when my own son smiled at me for the first time. I felt I *had* to pick him up and cuddle him. It was something over which I had no control. His smile left me no choice.

When your baby smiles, he is sharing something with you that no one else can. It is his gift to you. He is letting you know you are important in his life. Until now, you may have doubted your importance. You may have wondered whether you made any difference to him at all. You wondered if he would even notice if you weren't there. But your baby himself clears away all your doubts. He reaches out to you with his smiles, and later his cooing and laughter, acknowledging your existence and giving it meaning.

We are all eager to have a response from our infants as soon as possible. The earlier this occurs, the more we feel a part of his ongoing development. The enthusiasm of this process is seen in the words of an English father who felt that the eye movements of his three-day-old child were a specific communication to him:

"He was sleeping yesterday and his eyes were closed, and as I looked over he opened them. I moved away and he closed them. And I moved back again—and he opened them. Now I don't know what that is, maybe some kind of telepathy or something, but I just think he knew I was standing over him and he opened his eyes . . . it felt wonderful. This is the closeness that you have with a child, knowing that he feels his father standing over him and he opens his little eyes although he can't see anything."[3]

You can expect your child to start smiling directly at you, and at the sound of your voice, at about six to eight weeks. I did all kinds of things to elicit a smile from Jonathan. I tickled him, swung him back and forth, and bounced him on my leg. If that didn't get a smile, I would touch his face and talk and sing to him. Whistling, I soon found, was another effective way to get him to smile. Often I spent long periods of time experimenting with holding him in different positions that would trigger a grin. Sometimes I felt like a trained seal, doing anything for a smile. One of his favorite positions was to be held over my head while I was lying on my back. Hovering over me, he frequently drooled a large blob of saliva on my face, but I could tolerate that if he rewarded me with a smile.

You may have the same happy experience with your own growing infant. When you walk in the door at night, your baby's face lights up in a grin and you sense your tension and fatigue falling away. His smile sweeps away the preoccupations and concerns of the day. There is truly magic in a baby's smile. It is as if he is in touch with the forces of life and death and has not had an opportunity to become contaminated by the demands of society. His responses are those of raw energy, drives and impulses, and yet even at this primitive stage he is able to bestow upon us the ultimate gift of love—his smiles, coos, and laughter. These are like little treasures that we shall cherish for all time. For we are here in touch with a unique and creative fountainhead of life.

Just as your baby gives to you, you too can share with him. It's a two-way street, and you have much to offer. The more varied and diverse your ways of sharing and being with your child, the more intense will be the relationship and the more fun there will be for both of you.

Singing to your newborn is a unique way of sharing yourself. In reaching out to him with your voice, you are developing a particular way of relating to him, and this will be especially helpful to you during the first two months of his development, when he appears to be less responsive. As you sing a special song to him, it will eventually come to be "his song." He will begin to associate the song with his father, and later in his development he will experience a sensation of being loved and cared for whenever he hears his tune. His delight will be boundless when he hears you singing as you walk in the door. By the time he is two or three months old, he will start cooing in rhythm to your song as if he were singing along with you, and he may even giggle and let out what sounds like a shout or gurgle of delight.

I first began singing to Jonathan when he was one week old as a way of talking to him, and later when he was two months old to get him to coo back to me. I almost always sang "Twinkle, Twinkle, Little Star." It was a melody that my mother had sung to me. Partially to keep my interest perked and also to communicate my feelings to Jonathan, I would make up different lyrics such as "Twinkle, twinkle, little star, how Daddy loves his Jonathan are!" Frequently the words would be nonsensical, but it amused me and I found it a challenge to think of new verses. I sensed that Jonathan liked his song. And no one else could duplicate the way I sang it because no one else could sing it quite as distinctively off-key as I could.

Later, when Jonathan was four years old, I was to learn how significant that particular song was for him. He frequently wanted me to play monster with him, but at times, when my acting was too vivid, he would stop me for a moment or two to regain his equilibrium before urging me on again. On one occasion, instead of stopping me he began singing "Twinkle, Twinkle, Little Star" at a rapid clip. It was as if the tune had become so tied to a sense of care and safety that he could conjure up that feeling within himself by singing the song. The words themselves were like a security blanket, protecting him from harm in the outside world.

Find your own song, or even a little phrase or poem, that you can share with your newborn. Allow yourself to make up rhyming strains and think up new verses that are directed to your baby. The more nonsensical your words, the more spontaneous and natural you will be in the way you relate to him. As you sing to your baby, you will be allowing your own childlike playfulness to surface and you will feel more relaxed and more in touch with yourself.

Start singing to your baby early in his development, from the moment you see him, from the moment of birth. You can even sing to your baby during the pregnancy. Singing is a way of expressing vitality, a love of life, and a relatedness to the world around you. And later as you sing to your infant, his coos back to you will enhance the positive energy of your songs and deepen the bond between you. If you let yourself go, you will be surprised at the flexibility of your responses to your child. Dance with him, moving in rhythm to the music as he squeals with delight. Bounce him on your knee. These games of motion and others that you think up are exciting for your baby and will elicit coos, smiles, and giggles.

Infants are especially responsive to play with their fathers. In examining father and mother interactions with their eight-month-old infants, Dr. Michael Lamb noted that the fathers held their infants when they were playing with them, while the mothers in general held their infants more for caretaking functions than for play. As a result, the infants had a more positive response to any physical contact with their fathers. They also responded more positively to play with their fathers than with their mothers, perhaps because it was more physical and idiosyncratic.[4] So holding your baby and playing games of motion are especially important to him.

If you play a musical instrument, play to your child. Compose a special melody for him. Some fathers write songs for their children and sing to the accompaniment of a guitar. These songs talk about their fascination with their baby and their feeling of joy at his birth, describing how beautiful he is.

In an earlier chapter I mentioned a father who composed a song for his child in the bonding room. He later sang it to her frequently and felt he was creating a relationship through it. He said:

> "It was the first song! I made up a verse of it right there. It was my bonding song. In some way, the energy (of engrossment) was poured into it. Because even when I was driving home that night, I was preoccupied with that song and my child. It was like I was creating a relationship, or

creating an experience or trying to define it or make sense out of it somehow for myself."

Bonding songs are also love songs, a way of saying "I love you" to music. And the act of singing it, or setting the words to the emotional language of music, makes them even more powerful. These songs are not all that difficult to think up. Just speak your thoughts out loud. You could sing something like the following verses that were inspired by Jonathan:

He is so cute,
I love him so.
He crawls all around the room,
Look at him go!
When he cries I feel like I want to run,
But when he smiles, the sky opens up.
Then I know I love him, that's my son!

Or you could sing something like these verses which, although written by me, are derived from the enthusiastic words of fathers, describing their love for their baby girls.

Who would ever believe
That I could feel so much love
For a little baby girl
So soft, so lovely, like a dove.
She gurgled and cooed until I saw her,
Then she greeted me with a great big smile.
How I love her, that's my daughter!

Actually, singing is only one of many different ways of communicating with your baby. You can also share your thoughts and feelings with him. If you are upset or concerned about something, tell him about it. You can almost believe he understands as he coos and smiles at you in response.

It is important for fathers, and for that matter for all parents, to talk with their newborns. Some days your feeling might be, "Gee, I don't know what to talk to him about." Talk to him about anything, about his nose or his mouth, his toes or his tummy. Talk to him about the scenery, the trees, and the sky. Talk to him about the people you see, the voices you hear. Tell him about yourself, about your fears and your joys. Talk to him about how you feel when he smiles, and tell him what you feel about the color and power of his eyes that gaze on your face, and the beginning movements of his arms in your direction. If you feel a sudden surge of emotion, an engulfing feeling of love, share that with him. I have no doubt that he will feel embraced and nurtured by the intimate quality of the atmosphere around him.

It's amazing what nonsensical things you can say to your infant and how good you can feel in saying them. As your baby puts you in touch with the child within you, you begin to see a carefree, natural aspect of yourself emerge. You have and yet have not yourself become a child. This child is an aspect of the parent, and it is the integration of these two sides that plays a large part in your ability to relate to your infant while at the same time carrying on the day-to-day responsibilities of providing and caring for him.

Really, you can say anything to your tiny infant, share any of the intimate details of your life, and rest assured that he will not reject you. Not only that, he will always maintain confidentiality. And you can hum or sing almost any song, no matter how off-key or how many words you remember, and he will treat it with respect. This is the wonderful thing about newborns; they are so accepting. If only we could be as accepting of them—that's the challenge.

This sense of acceptance is the key to your ability to develop true sharing with your baby. For it means appreciating him in the here and now. Not as you had fantasized he would be, or as you imagine he will be, but rather how he is now. It is his active response that will draw you along this path of sharing.

In my own case, I knew my relationship with my two-month-old son had progressed when I stopped worrying about whether or not he spit up on me. I held him close to me, oblivious to whether I might get urine or stool on my clothes, although it was not something I anticipated with any eagerness. I could even handle changing his bowel movements without difficulty as long as I got a smile or two in return. Similarly, you will realize you are accepting "all" of your child when you accept the possibility that he might innocently make you the recipient of the contents of his various orifices. It seems a small price to pay when you get so much in return!

This is the beginning of true companionship, where you and your child now begin to share with each other spontaneously. There is an electricity in the air and a powerful feeling of hookup. The aura of intimacy is so intense that the memory of it will probably always remain with you.

In your companionship you may find yourself, almost without thinking, repeating to your new baby those things your own parents said to you when you were a child. Some of the phrases I recite to Jonathan were said to me by my father as far back as I can remember. When he was happy he used to leap into the air and say, with a great deal of excitement, "Yickel Pickel, katcha motch, lemonedy pie." Of course, I never knew what it meant, but it filled me with a sense of joy. And as a father, when I was happy I found myself reciting those words to my own baby. Later, when I would say "Yickel Pickel" to a Jonathan grown to nearly four, he would reply with a big smile, "Katcha motch."

In giving to your child in the way your parents gave to you, you experience a sense of history with him. If you experienced a relative void or absence of affection in your childhood, you can give your child the love and affection you missed. And when you do this, there is a healing. For as you give to your child, on another level you are also giving to yourself. The sense of historical roots is a unique part of sharing with your child, particularly as he becomes old enough to understand your words. Then you can begin to share past memories, not only of your experiences with him but experiences with your own parents—his grandparents—as well as his great-grandparents.

Being a part of your child's history allows you to have an entirely different and novel experience with him. You remember your fascination at seeing him born and the first time you held him, looked him in the eye, and were engrossed in him. You remember his first smiles, the times when all of you played together as a family, how you laughed and perhaps cried together in joy and even in frustration, and the sense of closeness you had with your wife and baby.

Share these experiences with your child as he develops. Tell him about the conversations you had when he was a baby, how he cooed in time to your voice. Tell him about the walks you had together, how you cared for him and played with him. As you share these memories, he will sense your excitement and joy, and later the rootedness of his past. As you hug and cuddle him while telling these stories when he is older, he will sense the continuum of your acceptance. Your love, like a warm and peaceful glow, will become a vital flame that nourishes him, a flame that will always exist in him long after you are gone.

When there are other siblings, they too can have a chance to hear and tell their own stories, their memories of their sibling's entrance into their lives, their fascination and love, and perhaps their anger and jealousy. The recounting of all of these sentiments in an atmosphere of love allows brothers and sisters to begin to transcend jealousy and anger and to experience one another in a positive way.

The story of your child's birth and development is of course unlike any other tale. It is filled with excitement, joy, and anguish. As you and your wife share these early experiences with your child, storytelling time becomes an intimate period that is shared by the entire family. I started talking to Jonathan about his birth and the earlier experiences I had had with him when he was about two years old. I was fascinated by the way he seemed hypnotized by Claudia's account of the pregnancy and birth, and I decided to try to share my own stories about him. I don't think he comprehended what I was saying intellectually, but my voice seemed to soothe and relax him. What was most important, I believe, was that I was expressing my own experience of love for him. And I think he must have sensed that.

Later, when he was three and four years of age, we told him about his birth and our earlier memories with him in more detail. Claudia would say: "When Mommy and Daddy found out that Mommy was pregnant with you, we were very excited. And then you began to grow in Mommy's tummy. You began to GROW and GROW and GROW and then you were BORN!"

And then I would say: "And Daddy jumped up and down and yelled, 'It's a boy, it's a boy, it's a boy!' And Mommy and Daddy hugged each other and were happy and loved you right from the beginning. And Daddy used to take you for walks. He carried you in the backpack. And Daddy sang 'Twinkle, Twinkle, Little Star' to you and talked to you about the trees and meadows, and you would smile and talk back with Daddy. Daddy loved to carry you on his back for walks and you would smile and clap your hands together when you got ready to go. Sometimes you tried to crawl into the backpack by yourself."

As you share this unique storytelling time, you can cuddle together as a family. You and your wife can take turns recounting the events of the past. And your youngster will probably ask you to repeat them again and again as he lies back with a big, beaming smile, enthralled.

As a doctor and a father I find that one of the intriguing aspects of jamily storytelling is that both parents are interacting with the child at more or less the same time but in their own individual styles. This is a wonderful example of the richness for the child of having both a mother and father. For each contributes something to him. Dr. Brazelton has confirmed that mothers and fathers generally talk and relate to their children from birth in unique and often contrasting ways.[5] The infant responds differently to each of his parents, with neither parental style being "better" than the other.

I noticed that Claudia and I each had our own individual style of relating to Jonathan. She sang and talked slower, more melodiously, and in a softer tone of voice. Jonathan often became excited and let out a high-pitched cry as she talked and sang to him. I tended to speak louder in a more staccato fashion, and I sang faster-moving songs. And his responses to me were quieter.

It is extremely important for the child to have these kinds of contrasting experiences with two different parents, not just in storytelling but in all kinds of activities—talking, singing, playing, or any kind of caretaking. These interactions enhance the child's physical and emotional development.

The lack of a father-child bond can be devastating to a child. Professionals who study such things have noted increased anxiety, juvenile delinquency, and emotional disturbance among father-deprived children.[6] In my own work, on countless occasions I have witnessed the destructive impact of the absence of a strong father-child bond: adolescents mourning the love they missed but are frequently unable to ask for and now often have difficulty accepting; children and adolescents who appear depressed, isolated, and lost, who cry out in the night, "Daddy, love me," and hearing no answer, turn their rage on themselves and others in episodes of alcohol and drug abuse, suicide attempts, fire-setting, stealing, assault, and even homicide.

The early months of a child's development can be an especially important and significant time for you to make contact, to begin sharing. Sometimes a special kind of effort is necessary. You need to be aware of your feelings, of your tendency, for example, to withdraw after a hard day's work. This is when you need to make a conscious decision to make contact. And as you gradually begin to experience the joy of sharing and playing, you will sense a "letting go" inside yourself. When this occurs, your ability to shift gears despite your exhaustion, to enter the world of the newborn and later of your growing child, will be vastly changed.

The opportunity to spend time alone with your baby is truly a privilege. It is a unique, perhaps even a spiritual, experience. There is a new sense of meaning in entering into a world of spontaneity with the infant. He helps us to escape the insidious erosion of ourselves that is forced upon us by the rational demands of our technological society. Our baby keeps us human and helps us to become more firmly rooted to the earth.

•14•

Holding Time

As part of growing up in a Western culture, we fathers tend to have an inferiority complex about our ability to relate to and care for our infant children. This complex is related to the notion that fathers are not supposed to get too involved. It is a point of view that varies with different cultures and is currently in a state of flux in the Western world. For example, in Sweden an increasing number of fathers are staying home and caring for their infants while their wives work. The state even encourages fathers to stay home after the birth of a child by providing parents with up to seven months' paid job leave which husband and wife can divide any way they see fit.[1] This sort of change is gradually occurring in the United States, but it is still so rare as to be considered novel. However, an increasing number of fathers are interested in the opportunity to be a part of the labor and birth of their children.[2]

The evolution of changes in parenting attitudes, strategies, and techniques means that there are varied and even conflicting influences impinging on us as parents. Becoming aware of these forces helps us as fathers to feel comfortable in taking an active role with our infants.

There are many who argue that we need to restructure our society to make it more attentive to the needs of parents. I certainly agree with this. For example, present-day work schedules make it extremely difficult for working parents to be a responsive and ongoing part of their children's lives. I feel that work schedules should be restructured to ensure not only economic efficiency but the well-being of the family as well. This would not only allow parents to find the gratification and financial security that comes from successful occupational pursuits but also allow them to be an integral part of the lives of their infants and growing children.

Obviously this revolution in our cultural orientation is not likely to occur overnight. This being the case, it is essential that we pay attention to what we fathers can do within the confines of our present culture. One of the most significant things a father can do is simply plan a certain period of time each day for holding his child. The allotment of this time is important not only in your child's development but in your own as well. Holding is something that you can do despite your occupational demands and the pressures of time. You can make holding time a reality in your life with even brief periods of fifteen or thirty minutes, although an hour or so is desirable if you can manage it. Do this for your own pleasure, and for what it will mean to both of you later.

It's extremely important that you get your holding time in every day, whether you have to get up thirty minutes earlier or go to bed a half hour later, and it matters not whether you do it while walking with your little girl, changing her, bathing her, or feeding her. It may be true that you haven't got the time to spare. Yet if we were absolutely required to learn a new task as part of our jobs, to come to work earlier or stay later, we would do it. It is essential to give equal emphasis to time for contact with our children. This is something we need each and every day, just as we require air to breathe. Contact breathes life into our relationship with our children and makes it come alive, grow, and mature.

The neglect of holding time reverberates far beyond this immediate period. It haunts us later with its "should haves" and "could haves." How many times have I heard fathers talk of their sadness and regret at not having been part of their children's lives. "If only I could do it over," they say. "Now it's too late." I tell these fathers that it is never too late; wherever they are with their child, they can begin now to foster that ongoing contact. But beginning in infancy, with your newborn, will ultimately have the greatest meaning for both of you.

You may argue that you were present at your child's birth, and you felt excited and hooked up with her from the start. You spend little time with her now, but you feel good about being a father. Isn't that enough?

No, it's not enough. It's not enough if you no longer maintain contact with her. The existence of a relationship early does not alter the fact that it goes underground if neglected. So while the relationship still exists as a potential, the lack of everyday contact results in your child's no longer perceiving her father as a reality. She has no way of knowing your feelings, your enthusiasm about fatherhood. You have to translate these feelings into a physical relationship in order for an impact to occur. Your relationship to your child needs a reality base, and this reality base is contact. This means not only touching, but much more. "Being in touch" is perhaps closer to the meaning I wish to convey. It means being in the physical presence of your infant, seeing her and letting her see you. It means listening to her, her gulps, gurgles, and coos, and watching her play. And it means hugging, holding, touching, fondling, snuggling, cuddling, playing with, swinging, and caressing her. It means having conversations with her as well as feeding and diapering her. In short, contact means your total physical experience with your baby, as opposed to your thoughts and images of her. It is through physical experience that you communicate your love for her, and it is in this way that she comes to know you.

How can fifteen minutes, even an hour, be meaningful? It's still your wife who spends most of the time with the baby. How can you make any impact? It's the way you hold her, the quality of the time, that has its effect on both of you. Even a few minutes of holding every day, when you are really focused on her, is likely to result in a continuation and reinforcement of your relationship. Some time is better than nothing. Give something. If you give nothing, despite your loving feelings there will be nothing.

Be absorbed with and concentrated on your baby when you hold her. When you do this, your body language communicates your awareness and appreciation of her uniqueness. She is bathed in an ambience of love and acceptance. Her response even accentuates the atmosphere of intimacy. And beyond your immediate shared pleasure, as you make yourself a real, living part of your infant's world that she can touch and feel, she begins to respond to you and remember you—and to be delighted when you are there.

As you find this holding time to be increasingly enjoyable, you may want to extend it for longer periods. You are hooked now; somehow you'll find time to be with your baby just because it feels good. It's amazing how we find time to do those things we enjoy, even when there is no time.

When Jonathan was about eight weeks old, I had become preoccupied with my studies in preparation for my board examinations in psychiatry, and as a result I had not spent much time with him for several days. I was at the library studying when I began to experience the most acute holding hunger you can imagine. I missed Jonathan, and I had to hold him. This feeling was so strong that it was almost as if it were a force over which I had no control.

Although I still had a lot of work to do, I headed for home, where I found Jonathan in a tearful state with our babysitter. "Your son's been bad," she said. "He's been crying all day." Jonathan was, in fact, hollering intensively. I placed him over my shoulder, a position he seemed to like, and headed into the fields behind my house as I chatted with him and sang "Twinkle, Twinkle, Little Star." Within fifteen minutes I noticed a stillness. I looked up at Jonathan, and he was fast asleep. I took him home and placed him in his cradle. There I lingered for some minutes looking at the grin that now appeared on his face in sleep.

I felt buoyed up by both the pleasure of our contact and his rapid response to me. I had held him for no more than a quarter of an hour. And in less than an hour, I was back at the library feeling rejuvenated. My parenting battery had been run down, and I had recharged it. A parent who is constantly with the infant requires breathing time to recharge his or her parenting battery. But a parent who is often away requires closeness. So your opportunities for contact are another type of spark that keeps your parenting battery going.

This experience of time together is even further enhanced when you have skin-to-skin contact with your baby. Your child perceives not only with her eyes and ears but also through her skin, the largest potential area of contact between parent and infant. And it is through hugging, holding, snuggling, touching, stroking, tickling, feeding, diapering, and bathing your child that physical contact is made, skin to skin.

It was as a necessary expedient that I discovered the significance of skin-to-skin contact. Because of all the splashing when I bathed Jonathan, I always got soaking wet. Finally, in frustration, I began taking off my shirt when I bathed him. It was then I discovered the exquisite pleasure of being in contact with his velvety soft skin.

You are literally closer when you are skin to skin. The normal movement and tactile contact with the infant are now exaggerated as your skin senses your baby directly rather than through clothing. Skin-to-skin contact is another level of communication, a basic level that strengthens the parent-infant bond without words.

When you snuggle your baby against you, skin to skin, you feel like your baby's protector. You enjoy sensing her chest against yours, her fingers on your face, the delightful softness of her buttocks, the soles of her feet, and her little toes. And when she grabs your finger, it's as if she's shaking your hand, reaching out to you in a special way. You feel very loving and tender toward her. So coo and sing to her. And when she gets sleepy, she might like to doze a bit on your chest.

Moments of genuine affection and intimacy are rare experiences in our lives. Holding time carries these rewards.

•15•

Portapouch and Backpack: Carrying Your Baby

"I had the feeling with the pack that it is nice to do something that she really likes. It's a way that I can really be close to her. I love to walk, and I love to be outside with her, and I like to move quickly. So it has just been a great experience; she loves it and I love it."
—Words of a first-time father describing carrying his baby on his back during her first year.

As part of your holding time, taking walks with your baby is an exciting opportunity for closeness. It is truly a bonding experience. For as you are walking with your little boy, you are focusing on him and experiencing the closeness of contact with him.

You won't be able to walk very far just carrying your baby in your arms because as he becomes increasingly restless he is likely to break out into piercing cries that send you running for cover, as if there were cannons exploding overhead. This native force is devastating. You need a means of carrying your infant for prolonged periods of time, a method that will keep your baby content and you in relative comfort. The answer initially is a baby sling, which you can begin using the first or second week after the baby arrives home. After a few months, when your child gains better head and neck control and can sit up, you can replace this with a backpack baby carrier

♦ Portapouch: The Front Baby Carrier

The front baby carrier is the single most effective tool that you can use with your baby during the first four to five months after his birth. This kind of carrier is universal.[1] Many different cultures have hand-fashioned infant carriers similar to those commercially available in the United States.

The front baby carrier is a kind of portable pouch—a "porta-pouch"—that allows you to carry your infant close to your chest and abdomen. The baby generally faces you, which gives you a good view of his face as you walk along. This infant sling was probably originally developed for mothers to give them increased flexibility and freedom. It certainly does this, for carrying the baby in the pouch frees your hands and allows you to do whatever other work you need to do while carrying the infant.

But the truly miraculous thing about the front baby carrier is that the rhythmic motion transmitted through walking has a calming effect on the baby, even soothing his crying. Many fathers are frustrated and exasperated by their infants' apparent lack of response to them in the early months. When you don't receive reinforcement from your child, the natural tendency is to back off and withdraw. But when you use the infant carrier, and your baby responds by stopping his crying, you know you can be effective and competent with your child. This greatly enhances your linkup with him.

Your walks with your little baby are like an adventure. Try to find a peaceful setting to walk in—a beach, a lake, a park, a field, a forest. The tranquillity of the setting enhances the enjoyment of your walk even if you have to drive to get there. If there are no parks, fields, or beaches around, just take a walk in your neighborhood. Walk around the block, or walk to a friend's house. This gives you an opportunity to not only enjoy your baby's presence but also to show him off.

Although you may initially feel anxious about walking with the baby in the portapouch, after a few minutes your nervousness will decrease considerably. If you are in a quiet place, you may even become aware of your infant's breathing rhythm. It almost seems in synchrony with your own breathing. If your baby is crying when you first set out, don't worry. Just continue walking. If you know that he has recently had a feeding, that his diaper is not soiled or wet, that a safety pin is not sticking him, and that he is not sitting on a sharp or hard object, then you can rest assured that there's no other problem. His cries will gradually subside as you walk. And when he stops crying you will feel surprised and pleased. You may say to yourself, "He's never responded like that to me before; he's never even acted like I exist."

As you walk along together, place your arms around his back and embrace him. Feel his hair, stroke his head, his arms and legs. Notice how soft his skin is. Place your finger into his hand, and you will enjoy seeing how it closes around yours. Your newborn is acknowledging your presence in his own way, and you feel increasingly proud.

My own first experience with the portapouch came when Jonathan was thirteen days old. I remember the sense of adventure as I set out with him into one of the canyons that crisscrosses the area of San Diego that we live in. As I headed downward, it was hard to believe that a technological world lay so near, for I felt as if I were descending into a hidden realm of nature and perhaps being transported back in time and place.

In the peacefulness of the canyon, my mind began to play. Compelling images flashed before me. I was an Indian warrior carrying his newborn son into the wilderness for his first experience with Mother Earth. I was his protector and his guardian spirit. I felt a sudden power that would ward off all intruders and prevent any harm befalling us as long as we remained together. Strange scenes appeared before my eyes: A lion charged and I fought him off in violent hand-to-hand combat before finally destroying him. I whisked my child away from a deserted beach, and with the speed of a gazelle outraced a huge tidal wave that threatened to crash upon us. Images of thunder and lightning, mountains, valleys, oceans, and lakes rushed through my mind. No, this was not an afternoon walk into a small canyon in the middle of San Diego but an entry into a secret crevice in the earth that carried me into a world of mystery and magic.

Your baby will probably be asleep in a short time, despite all the drama going on around him. As you look at his face and touch his hand, which is now flopping in the air, you may feel a sense of wonder that you and your wife could have created this unique human being who is so perfect. You may exclaim out loud, "Where did you come from? It's just unbelievable. It's hard to believe that we created you."

This sense of wonder often begins the moment a father first sees his child. As one father told me about his son's birth:

> "There was a lot of sense of 'this is miraculous!' The fact that he could come out and be perfect. I remember looking at his hands and seeing the fingers and the fingernails. Everything was so perfectly formed. And just thinking about what are the odds of somebody, of a baby, happening like this. What an incredible miracle it is that nature works this way."

As your infant sleeps, he may slump down in the sling so that he is not readily visible. You may only know that he is there by the warmth and weight of his body, and by his hands, which are locked around yours. His presence is something shared between the two of you, an intimate secret until he finally reveals his place of concealment with a cry, grunt, or sudden movement.

During this kind of closeness with your newborn, you can begin to associate your portapouch with a kangaroo pouch. It is as if the pouch is a part of your body and your baby is inside. And when the sack sinks to the level of your abdomen, it is as if it has become a womb. In the peaceful calm of your baby's slumber you may not be immediately certain whether you are carrying him inside or outside your body—or perhaps it is both!

Some men feel alarmed by the intense feelings they experience as they carry their baby close to them, especially if they have fantasies of themselves as having a womb and being pregnant. But don't be alarmed. It's perfectly natural and normal for a man to fantasize about being pregnant. Many men, during their wives' pregnancies, have shared with me the experience of imagining themselves as pregnant, or wishing they too had the opportunity to carry the baby like their pregnant wives. The use of the baby carrier probably allows those images to surface to a greater degree because of the intense, close contact.

Carrying such a young baby may seem strange to you at first. Yet you may also feel a sense of excitement and accomplishment. The fact that you are secluded together, that at this moment he depends on you for his entire existence, enhances the intimacy. Despite his young age and your lack of experience, it's all up to you.

As the days pass and you continue to be successful in carrying your baby and soothing his cries on these walks, you will increasingly feel more self-confident and competent in your role as a father. You may feel like showing off your newfound ability as a parent. At times you may feel like shouting out to the world, "Look at me—I'm a father!" "Look at my son," or "Look at my daughter." These are unique moments, truly gifts of life.

When you carry your child next to you as you meander along, you'll be amazed how people come up to you. There's something about a father carrying a little baby that fascinates people. It's not just that it's a baby but that your experience of love and connection with your child is felt by people around you. Sometimes people will want to touch your baby, even if he is asleep. Men will frequently stop to talk to you about their own children. You will also find yourself much more aware of babies in general, stopping people on the street to ask them about their children, inquiring enthusiastically, "When did he start smiling and sitting and walking?" And you may suddenly be more understanding of the crying outbursts of your friends' children—in contrast to your prefather days.

The baby carrier gives you an enormous sense of freedom that you would otherwise not have. Even though the baby may have curtailed your personal independence, and you and your wife can no longer come and go whenever you wish, with the portapouch you can still get out of the house and be active. Just dress your child for the weather, put him into the carrier, and take off. This is particularly helpful if you are a mobile person—if you enjoy walking, hiking, jogging, and running—and have a hard time remaining at home. Walking with your baby is a new dimension, an activity that the two of you can enjoy together.

During Jonathan's first year of life I was studying and traveling in Europe. I used to take him for walks just after it snowed, and I would point out the different shapes made by the snow crystals as the sun glistened on them. We would often drive to different places for our walks, which increased the sense of novelty and exploration for me and, I think, for Jonathan. Sometimes Claudia would join us and it would be a kind of family outing.

The freedom and flexibility the infant carrier provided allowed us to make numerous excursions. We traveled to the tops of high mountains and then hiked down, Jonathan enjoying the scenery all the while. And we walked through different towns, exploring the smells, sights, and sounds of new locations.

The use of the baby carrier can become "your thing." It gives you a specific activity with your child, which alleviates the feeling common to so many young fathers of standing around with their hands in their pockets while their wives take care of the baby. It also gives you a way of helping out in the early months when the baby's crying may make you and your wife feel as if you are in the grip of an ever-tightening vise. When your wife says, "Get him out of the house! Take him for a walk! Do anything to stop his crying!" you'll be eager for this opportunity to be alone together.

Although it is the rhythmic back-and-forth motion of walking that soothes and comforts your baby, I believe that the carrier gives the baby a sense of well-being in another way as well. The sling places the baby's body across the left side of your chest, in close proximity to your heart. There are many researchers who comment on the calming effects of the infant's being held next to the heart. They suggest that the heart's regular action helps reestablish the infant's inner equilibrium. Perhaps, too, it is a throwback to the secure environment of the womb, when the pulsating actions of the heart were a constant background to the infant's existence.

♦ Backpack

The companionship that develops as you carry your baby in his sling is further enlarged upon when he is older and you begin to use the baby backpack. This is a cloth-and-metal infant seat that fits onto your back like a camping backpack. The seat gives your baby an opportunity to look at the world from your shoulders.

You may experience some sadness when your youngster first begins to give up the body sling. You notice that he's beginning to put up a fight more and more, letting you know that he does not like the restraint of the sling. He wants to face the world, to see what is happening. After you get over your initial feelings of loss, you'll begin to realize that the backpack provides an opportunity for another type of relationship.

The backpack can usually be used from four or five months, when your baby has beginning muscular control of his head and neck, until he is a year or so of age. At around one year, he will be taking his first steps, and he will be less and less inclined to enjoy sitting in the backpack as he learns to walk on his own. But now, while your infant is in the backpack, he is facing the world for the first time. In the front carrier, he was facing you. Now he is more independent. Increasingly he is smiling, cooing, gurgling, and babbling in response to you and to the environment around him. This sense of independence yet continued closeness is captured in these words:

> "She loves being there. She is a student of the world, is looking around and is interested in new things—different sights, different sounds. She loves animals. She loves little babies. The backpack gives her the freedom to move a little, as opposed to the stroller or holding her. She loves this, as it gives her independence, yet also raises her up and provides her with the closeness and security that I imagine she feels good about."

It may be hard to see your baby when he's in the backpack, but you can turn around and pat his arm, look at his face, and exchange smiles. You'll see his reflection in store and car windows, and you may even exchange messages. Says one father:

> "What I do is stop in front of car windows and look in. It takes him a while to register, but often he'll see his face, and that brings delight. Sometimes he sees me, and we exchange these smiles through the car window—it's really nice."

♦ The Companionship of Walking Together

As you walk along with your baby, whether in the portapouch or the backpack, your feeling of closeness merges with a sense of protectiveness. You feel your own strength and power; and you may say to yourself, "I'll protect my baby no matter what. Nobody would dare hurt him. . . ." With intensifying companionship with your child, you feel a joy and a peaceful acceptance of your place in the total realm of things. As one father stated:

> "There is a feeling of manliness and of strength. I feel my age and I feel a maturity, my place in the universe, that things are right in the world."

You are now beginning to experience a true acceptance of your new fathering role. Your child's responses and his acknowledgment of you will enhance your sentiments toward him. You feel increasingly engrossed. And you feel closer with each passing day. One father said:

> "It just feels right when I'm carrying her. A father's daughter. She looks up at Daddy and I feel that even more. I think about the time when I come home and she starts kicking and being excited. It is such a nice response—the trust. It is a great gift to have another human being respond to you in such a pure way."

The companionship is enhanced as you talk to your baby and share yourself with him. "There's a big dog. What a beautiful dog he is. Look at the truck going by—isn't that interesting?" Your enthusiastic response to the world around you will surely get him to perk up and take notice too. And when he sees something that startles him, you can let him know that there is nothing to be afraid of. You can do this by repeating, as you cuddle or stroke him, "Daddy is here, and everything is fine!"

I have said that walking in a natural setting heightens the intimacy of the experience, especially if you enjoy nature. You can share the natural wonder, the peace and harmony that you yourself feel—and you really do feel it. And your baby can share your joy and fascination for the processes of life.

Sometimes I walked along the ocean with Jonathan, and the sound of the waves created a scintillating, vibrating experience that interacted with the two of us. I felt as if we were part of nature—part of the sand and the earth, the waves and the ocean. We were a part of the seagulls shrieking overhead and part of the clouds above. Somehow I was no longer a mere mortal. We were a part of everything, and Jonathan was a part of me. We were spirits that had transcended our physical bodies. We were bound together, now and forever, by a love that was mystical yet rooted in the real world.

These walks with your child can be very creative moments. If you like to write prose or poetry, write down a few lines in a notebook, or carry a tape recorder and capture some of your feelings with it. Perhaps later you might want to share them with your child as he grows older. You'll be amazed at the kinds of creative ideas that come to you as you walk.

Your outings with your child will become special moments that you share together and both look forward to. It's important to protect this time from intrusion by disturbing thoughts or feelings. Just focus on your baby. Otherwise you may be there but your thoughts will be elsewhere. Clear your mind. Don't read while walking. And try not to focus on economic or domestic problems immediately before going out. It saps your energy and makes it more difficult to be available. Find a time of day when you are less preoccupied, when you feel less pressured about work and the constraints of time. Walking just before dinner is a good time, or walking on Saturday or Sunday mornings.

As pleasurable as these walks can be, there will of course be times when the infant carrier does not soothe your crying child. This rarely happens, but when it does you are likely to return home frustrated and angry. "How could he spoil the pleasure of our walk together?" you may ask. It is then that you realize how important the walks really are to you.

But in spite of occasional setbacks, your use of the portapouch and the backpack will be a key point in your relationship with your infant as well as your feelings about yourself as a man and father.

·16·

Secret Weapons

While the portapouch is an invaluable ally against the fury of your newborn's cries, there are times that it just doesn't perform its magic. And there are times when you're away from home and don't have it with you. Or times when it's too cold and rainy to take the baby outside in it. This is when you long for some secret counterweapon or technique to relax and soothe your crying baby.

Scene: You are arriving home from work. It's been a particularly rough day for your wife because your baby daughter has been crying up a storm. Your wife has been eagerly anticipating your arrival home. As you step in the door, she effects baby transfer so rapidly that you feel like the anchorman receiving the baton for the last leg of the relay. Perhaps you're already irritable and worn down by your workday and are not filled with enthusiasm for child care. Your wife is just glad you're home. She is trying to prepare dinner and has made a rapid exit with the words, "You take the baby, I'm going crazy!" And your baby, perhaps also experiencing the tension of this time of day, is howling.

With your newborn in tow, you're now trying to change your clothes and make some quick phone calls while somehow holding and responding to your baby. You feel as if you need three hands, because every time you put her down she howls louder. She wants to be held even though it doesn't stop her from crying, and as this accelerates you feel more and more angry, tense, frustrated, and incapable.

The *football* position is the secret weapon that meets your urgent need. Although it does not provide you with three hands, it allows you to hold your child comfortably with one. I became familiar with this position through a friend who as a new father had successfully employed the position with his own baby. He in turn had had it demonstrated to him by Dr. John Welsh, a fine, old-time pediatrician in San Diego.

In the football position, the infant is carried facedown, your forearm under her chest. Her legs straddle your arm. Your hand curls across near her mouth, and you can offer her a finger to suck on. It's not exactly like carrying a football, but it is similar. Your infant's opportunity to suck on your finger may be one of the key reasons for the success of this position.

The football position will be one of your most important secret weapons. Babies are frequently enthralled with being carried this way and will often stop crying. And your ability to hold your child with one hand allows you to use your other hand, for brief periods, to take care of other pressing matters, thus giving you increased capabilities.

Your friends and neighbors will be amused to see you carrying your child in this fashion. When I went walking outside with Jonathan in the football position my neighbors would jokingly say, "Whatcha got there, a bag of potatoes?" or, "You look like you've got a football there, Marty."

There are some variations on this position that you may find useful in your anticrying armamentarium. In the *forward pass* position, you hold your child precisely as in the football position but you use your arm like a seesaw, swinging it back and forth. The motion closely mimics an underhand forward pass. The rhythmic sensation is similar to that of a cradle or a rocker, and will probably soothe your infant. It certainly worked with Jonathan. From the time he was six weeks old, when I first started using it, until he was about three months old, the forward pass position almost always put him to sleep, that is, if I could keep it up long enough.

That, of course, is a real problem. Because you may not have sufficient strength to swing your baby for extended periods of time, you may prefer to use the *running-with-the-ball* position, the second variation. This involves walking while carrying your baby in the football position. Especially if you walk outdoors, where you can get a natural walking rhythm going. The motion is usually sufficient to calm your baby's cries and relax and soothe her, lulling her to sleep within thirty minutes. If you like to walk as much as I do, you'll enjoy the running-with-the-ball variation.

I remember when Jonathan was three months old and Claudia and I were picnicking with him at the beach. He was becoming fretful.

Claudia had just fed him and we knew he wasn't hungry, so I took him in the football position and walked the length of the beach with him. He comfortably sucked away on my index finger, and within a short time he was asleep. I hadn't realized that we might look a bit unusual until a woman came up to me and said she had never seen an infant sleeping so peacefully in such a strange position. She asked if she could take our picture, to which I consented. For me the important thing was that the position worked, and I didn't give a hoot how strange we looked or whether people argued that I shouldn't let my baby suck on my finger.

If you're concerned that your baby could fall from your forearm in the football position, then place your other hand over her back as you carry her on your arm, thus giving her extra support. You can reserve holding her one-handed for those times of absolute necessity. Actually, it's difficult if not impossible for an infant to slip out of your football position grasp, even one-handed, in the early months. But later, as she becomes increasingly mobile and able to start turning (four to eight months), greater caution is advised.

If you are going to use this position, it wouldn't hurt if you did some training in advance. The first time I carried Jonathan for two hours I felt as if my arms were going to fall off. My shoulders, forearms, and biceps were sore for days.

One way to train is to get some five- or ten-pound dumbbells and do curls with them ten times with each arm every day, or every other day, until you work up to fifty or a hundred a day. That would probably be effective in building up the strength of your arms. Of course, you may wind up being too fatigued from your workouts to carry your baby. So the easiest way to train is simply to carry your infant for short periods in the beginning and then for progressively longer periods. In this way your training allows you to spend your time in contact with your baby.

In using these carrying positions, be prepared to be a switch hitter. Alternate frequently between left and right hands. This allows each arm to get some rest so that your strength is not overtaxed. Another nearly-one-handed technique that will be useful is the *shoulder* position. Just lay your baby on her stomach across your shoulder, her feet hanging over your chest. She will lie there contentedly, while you gently steady her with your hand on her bottom or legs, letting her look around the room as you talk on the telephone or change your clothes. She looks so comfortable, as if she were meant to be there. When she grows heavy on one shoulder, shift her to the other. The only disadvantage of this position is that you can't see her face as she is facing backward. You'll really miss looking into her eyes and touching her smooth face and hair. But it is a practical position. And it gives you another weapon, another tool, that you can use with your infant.

You will find it advantageous to develop a variety of positions that soothe your child. Coping with a fretful or shrieking baby requires a flexible orientation. I think that flexibility is synonymous with being a parent. If one approach doesn't work, you try another. It is the continual testing out of weapons and strategies on the actual field of battle that allows us to know their worth. As you begin this testing process, you'll be surprised at how many different effective strategies you will discover.

The *basketball* position (or *chest-behind* position) is a case in point. In this position you place your right hand under your child's rear end, while your left hand provides support for her chest. In the *shooting basketball* position variation, you now raise the baby up and down, as if preparing to shoot the ball through the hoop. These two positions are helpful in quieting your child, but they do not give you as much mobility as the football positions. Also, it is more difficult to maintain the basketball positions for long periods, as they are a bit more awkward. Nevertheless, they are another effective option that you can try with your baby when she's crying or when you're feeling tired of carrying her in other ways.

The *knee-chest* position is another effective strategy. In this position the knees, head, and chest of the baby are brought closer together, replicating to some degree the folded position of the baby in the uterus. Rhythmically and slowly moving your baby up and down as she is enclosed in your arms in this position often reduces crying.

Another technique, which may work for some of the same reasons the knee-chest position works, is to swaddle your baby securely in a blanket. This is a technique used by some native Indian cultures. At times, when a newborn is howling, she stimulates herself further by the unrestrained moving around and jerking of her extremities. Swaddling gives her an increased sense of physical boundaries, which may result in reduced crying. Personally, I think it's nicer if the sense of boundaries can come in the contact with you. So try some of the other positions before you try swaddling. In this way you are having increased physical contact together. But swaddling or a lesser variation of it—just wrapping her snugly in a blanket—can be effective if all else fails. Also, you can't hold her all the time, and blanket wrapping may calm her sufficiently to allow her to sleep.[1]

While some babies are calmed by their bath, others are soothed by the sensual stimulation of the shower. So, particularly if you shower at the end of the day, you could try showering with your baby when you get home. Be sure the water is neither too hot nor too cold and that the spray is not too intense. Also, hold her snugly in your arms and talk and sing to her as you shower together and enjoy that skin-to-skin contact. Make sure you have a pad on the shower floor to prevent slipping. If the shower soothes her, or even if she is not crying and just seems to take pleasure in it, this is something that could become a regular ritual between you and your baby.

What soothes one infant, however, may not soothe another; and what works and feels right for one father may not be right for another. Additionally, what works early in the child's development may not be effective later; and a strategy that fails one month may become successful the next. So you'll want to find out what works for you and your own infant. This may very well be different from what seems to work between your infant and your wife. Each of us is different. In many ways we are like the image of the forest. There we can find a variety of different forms: big trees and little trees, oak trees and fir trees, trees that bend and those that don't. Every tree is unique and plays a significant part in the totality of the forest.

It is your increasing contact with your child that allows you to begin to read her feelings and become aware of her natural rhythms. And she will begin to recognize your touch, your voice, and your own rhythms. As she begins to associate you with the gratification of her needs, your very presence will come to have a soothing effect on her.

Try to be spontaneous and inventive in your use of soothing strategies with your child. When I took Jonathan for walks I would alternate carrying him in a number of different positions, particularly in response to his angry and irritable cries. These positions seemed to keep him happier while preventing me from getting overtired. For example, I might start out carrying him in the baby sling. If he got tired of that, I would put him over my right shoulder and then perhaps over my left shoulder. When either of us grew weary of that, I would carry him in the football position. As my arm became increasingly fatigued,

I would switch from left to right arms. Perhaps I would let him stand on my left hand and then on my right hand. If you alternate different positions and strategies, you may find you can carry your baby for several hours and keep him contented. And all of these different positions and strategies are confidence builders for you.

When effective counterweapons are available to relieve the bombardment of your newborn's cries, then a true linkage can take place. This is more than peaceful coexistence, it is the opportunity to hook up in a meaningful and loving fashion. You begin to experience a joy even in the so-called mundane situations of daily child care.

When I am alone with my son, the things I do with him carry a special significance. Something as commonplace as holding and feeding him, or having him fall asleep in my arms, carries a special significance for me. It is as if a unique, almost indescribable something begins to express itself—the link between father and child.

•17•

A Chapter for Mothers: Helping Fathers Hook Up

As a mother you can play a very significant part in helping your husband become engrossed in his new baby. But if the baby herself is so attractive to him, if her smiling and cooing have so much impact, why should you have to do anything more?

The answer is that many new fathers will not make the effort to get involved with their newborn infants until they feel they have permission from their wives. This doesn't mean they don't want to get involved. It means that most new fathers see the baby as their wife's staked-out claim, and they are reluctant to trespass on her territory.

Often the husband is responding to the reality of the situation. His wife is competent with the new baby, and he sees the strong relationship between them. In hanging back, it's as if he is saying to her, "You come first. It's your relationship with the baby that really counts." If his wife doesn't actively draw him into the circle, he is likely to continue hanging back, feeling unnecessary and unwanted. This is a common feeling among fathers that has been observed by a number of researchers. One study at Stanford University was done with a group of premature infants and their parents.[1] About a week before each of the babies was to be discharged from the hospital, a meeting was held with the parents in which they were encouraged to hold their infant as a prelude to their adjustment at home. The fathers literally stood back, waiting for their wives to take the babies. It was only after the mothers put the infants down and invited their husbands to hold them that they timidly attempted to do so.[2]

♦ Space Available

You need to let your husband know that there is a space available for him in the relationship with the baby. Your permission to him, that it is okay to be involved, is very important. You are in many ways like a catalyst, the necessary ingredient that allows him to experience his feelings about the baby, and thus to become engrossed. This issue of space available is basic to your husband's willingness to participate with his child.

In some families space is made available by the absence or unavailability of the mother to care for the child. The film *Kramer vs. Kramer* illustrated this point. In this drama the father was focused primarily on his work until the abrupt departure of his wife from the home. This created a massive space in relation to his child. He responded to that opening, becoming intensely involved and intimately bonded with his child.

A space available also occurs when a mother becomes ill and cannot care for the child. In response to this emergency most fathers will make special efforts to be more involved and assume more child-care responsibilities. As a consequence they usually feel closer to their children.[3]

If a woman works long hours at her job, this is another situation where there is a space available. In response to this, many men will adjust their work schedule to take a more responsible role, because they feel they have to. Nevertheless, in our culture it is still usually the mother who has the primary care of the child and the intense involvement, even if she also works outside the home. Unless the father's work allows him flexible time with his baby, how can he become involved and feel close to her—despite his wife's close and intimate relationship with her? There may appear to be no space available for him. But a woman can create a space by simply stepping back—by offering the child to her husband and letting him know how much she enjoys his contact with the baby.

When a father feels excluded from the mother-infant relationship, he usually deals with his discomfort by pursuing his work with greater intensity. He comes to regard the family economics as his territory, just as he sees the baby as his wife's territory. And the more intensely he pursues his occupational goals, the more vigorously his wife tends to involve herself with the baby. These two paths can lead the husband and wife away from each other. This course is difficult to break away from unless the partners can get a perspective on what is happening. If the wife is also working outside the home, their paths can become even more divergent.

Looking at your family as a whole, it might appear that your main focus on the baby and your husband's on work would be advantageous for all concerned. Each of you has your own sphere of influence Such an equitable division of labor should be an efficient way for the family to function.

Certainly in earlier cultures there was usually a very strict division of labor. While women stayed home, men went off to hunt, providing food for the survival of the family, the clan, and the tribe. And the father's prowess in the art of hunting and fighting ensured the family's continued existence despite intruders from outside.[4]

In our modern Western culture, however, we have passed beyond the point where we have to cope with physical survival alone. This is not to downplay the importance of the protective function—the providing of food, clothing, and shelter. There is no question that this is an important aspect of fathering (and of parenting in general). But in today's world we are talking about a different kind of survival: the survival of the family unit.[5] The family unit ideally should provide nurturing and support, while allowing autonomous growth of all its members. There should be a continually evolving intimacy between husband and wife, a positive bond between mother and child, and a hookup between father and child.

The real enemy of today's family is the gradual and insidious loss of intimate relationships. This can occur when a father focuses entirely on providing for his family or on amassing wealth. For when his focus becomes onesided, it throws off his emotional balance. He ignores and loses that other essential aspect of fathering, the nurturing side. The isolation and detachment experienced by such a father is very destructive. Not only does he feel a lack of involvement, participation, and contact with his growing child, but he often allows a wide chasm to open between himself and his wife.

This does not happen to all fathers, of course. Many need little encouragement to involve themselves with their young children. However, in my personal and professional experience, the vast majority of fathers are somewhat uncertain and anxious with their newborns. The average father does need a moderate degree of continuing support and encouragement from his wife to bring him into active contact with the baby. This is true even when his early contact with her was in a positive setting, such as being present at the birth.

There are also a small number of fathers who seem to have no real interest in the baby. They are perfectly content to have their wives take over all aspects of the infant's care. A woman must take an especially active role in getting this father involved. The longer he stays aloof from his infant, the harder it is for him to become involved later as the child grows older.

There is no way of knowing in advance how engrossed a father will be with his baby. Even his interest during the pregnancy and his presence at the birth do not mean he will automatically become involved.[6] However, if there is a space made available early—during the pregnancy and birth—he is much more likely to feel wanted and needed in the new family. This means that, ideally, he should be included in events from the very beginning: attending the doctor visits during the pregnancy, listening to the baby's heartbeat, attending childbirth education classes, and practicing coaching his wife in her breathing exercises. He should be encouraged to be at the delivery. If his wife doesn't ask him to be with her, he may not ask. And if she actually says she doesn't want him to be there, he is unlikely to go against her wishes. Not only that, he will develop rationalizations as to why this is the best course.

This state of affairs was strikingly illustrated in a conversation I had with an English father in his early twenties. He was present with his wife in the labor room and then left when she was ready to deliver their first child. He said:

> "I was with my wife through the whole of labor, and I felt like I wanted to go with her into the delivery room. I felt a little bit like I was cheated—I would have liked to see him born. But she didn't want me to be there. And it was just as well, you know, (pause) because she had twenty-one stitches."

There are events and circumstances during the birth, such as a difficult delivery or unsupportive hospital staff, that can cause a father to withdraw from the experience. But generally speaking, the more he participates before and at the birth, the more likely he is to become engrossed. Then, even if he later changes his focus and begins to involve himself intensely in his work, he can usually be more easily drawn back into the family again.

A father cannot hope to experience or receive love from his infants and growing children if his focus is primarily elsewhere. This fact is underlined by an interview I conducted with another young father immediately after the birth of his first child. When I asked if he loved his own father, he stopped a moment, seeming at first incredulous that I should ask such a silly question. Then he smiled and replied, "Well, I wouldn't say I loved him, (pause) but I respected him." He went on to talk about the absence of any meaningful contact between his father and himself. His father, although present in the home, was distant, taking the role of family provider and stern disciplinarian. This new father said that he wanted things to be different with his own child. This was the reason he had decided to be present at his child's birth, to start from the beginning.

This is the opportunity that the newborn provides, a chance to start fresh, to establish contact from the beginning. And here is where you as a woman can be instrumental. The challenge before you is not only that of appreciating your husband's desire to protect and preserve his family but of helping him to merge this with a sense of closeness with you and the baby.

♦ Drawing Fathers In

How can you let your husband know that there is a space available for him? How can you draw him in and help him hook up with the baby? Any early opportunity that he has to hold, touch, and carry the baby will be of great significance. Simply say something encouraging such as, "Isn't she beautiful? She's so much fun to hold. Why don't you try?" Communicate your own enjoyment and enthusiasm to him.

Be understanding if your husband feels tentative, awkward, and inadequate about holding a tiny baby. Above all, don't criticize. Remember how anxious you may have been when you first held the baby in the hospital, how sensitive you were to any comments made by hospital personnel that seemed unsupportive or depreciated your ability to care for your new baby. Remember how their lack of consideration may have upset you and made you angry. Your husband may be even more sensitive, and any critical remark you make may cause him to withdraw instantly. More than likely he will return the infant to you with some sort of mumbled comment about not being very good with babies. It might be another week or two before he's willing to make another effort. If you and your husband don't realize how powerful your negative comments can be, both of you may be perplexed by this withdrawal. So be encouraging. Perhaps you can even talk about the apprehension and uncertainty that you felt when you first held the baby (and perhaps even at times experience now). This may give him the boost he needs so that he will persevere.

After my own baby was born, my wife gave me a lot of support and encouragement. This was fortunate because I thought of her as commander-in-chief in matters that related to Jonathan. I tended to look to her for approval in anything I did with him, especially during the first two months when I was still rather unsure of myself. If he cried when I picked him up, or if I thought Claudia frowned or uttered the slightest sound of disapproval, I quickly returned the baby to her.

Like other fathers, I too allowed my relationship with my son to move backward during the early months. I was working hard at my job, so I saw him less. And because I had less contact with him, I became less confident about my ability to care for him. As a result, I felt more reluctant to pick him up and play with him. You can do a number of things to help your husband break out of this cycle, to enhance his relationship with his child. Support and encourage him to hold the baby, cuddle her, and play with her. If you are bottle-feeding, let him give her one of the feedings. Even if you are breast-feeding, your husband could feed her with a supplemental bottle if you are using one. Or he could feed her with your milk extracted by a breast pump.

Encourage him to interact with the baby in every way you can. Most important, encourage him to be spontaneous with her. Encourage him to coo, sing, and dance with the baby, for this is an emotional language that she understands. She will be likely to respond with her own unique facial expressions and body movements, and by smiling, cooing, and laughing.

Reinforce whatever response she makes when her father is present. When she smiles at him, say, "Look, she's smiling at you, honey." Or if she grabs his finger you could say, "Look, she wants to hold your hand." If she coos, you could say, "She's trying to talk to you." Point out how she gazes at him and how she opens her eyes when he enters the room. Point out how she may even mimic him in his expressions. You could say something like, "She's pursing her lips the way you do. Isn't that fascinating?" The more your husband sees the baby as an individual, with her own set of discrete responses, the more involved he will feel. And if he sees the baby responding specifically to him, this will have a tremendous impact.

I still remember how excited I was when Jonathan, at about three to four months, began reaching out to me when he saw me approach, and Claudia would say, "See how he knows his daddy!" These comments enhanced and underlined in my mind the importance of my contact with him. Claudia's emphasis on the significance of my relationship certainly let me know there was a space available and that her close relationship with Jonathan could also include me.

One of a father's most important opportunities for contact with the baby is when he arrives home from work. However, this may not always be an opportune time for you. If you have an outside job, your own schedule at coming-home time may require that you do certain things with the baby at certain times, which makes it difficult for her father to have contact with her unless he takes over some of those activities himself. His taking over for a while is a fine idea in any case, though it probably needs to be a gradual process.

But for the sake of discussion, let's say you are a mother who is home all day with the baby. Let's say you've had a tough day coping with her. She's been irritable, fretful, and just downright cranky. You feel on edge, and every time the baby cries it's as if a raw nerve has been irritated. On such a day you might well say to your husband as he walks in the door, "Don't touch the baby. I'm trying to get her to sleep." Unfortunately, there is nothing more damaging to a father's feelings and initiative with his baby than to be told, "Don't touch her." It implies that he's neither needed nor wanted. He's in the way.

It might seem unfair to you that your husband thinks he can just hop in, take over, and play with the baby when you've just succeeded in getting her off to sleep. It's the first peace and quiet you've had all day. And your husband comes in, saying loudly and enthusiastically, "Honey, I'm home," and the baby starts crying again. It's reasonable that you might feel angry.

But your husband has been mired in the frustrating world of external demands and economic necessities, and he's happy to be home. Hopefully, he wants to see and hold his baby. In the long run, the gains of his picking up the baby are much greater than the losses. A working father may have very little time to spend with his child, perhaps one or two hours a day. If you ask him not to touch her when she is asleep, whole days may pass during which he has little or no opportunity for contact. This in itself is likely to be much more disruptive than any potential crying.

If in fact the baby is usually asleep when her father comes home, and his picking her up is disruptive, consider changing the baby's schedule so that she is awake for his arrival and goes to sleep shortly afterward. Perhaps he can be the one to feed her her bottle (if she gets one) and then pat or rock her to sleep. Changing her schedule is done by gradually moving her feeding up or back until she becomes used to being awake about the time her daddy arrives. If you can accomplish this (and not all babies will oblige), it might resolve the problem of your husband's contact with her. And if you've just come home from work yourself, this routine may give you a few extra minutes to shift gears.

Be as flexible as you can about how, when, and where you and your husband should respond to the baby. Rigid expectations about these things will result in a loss of creative contact for both of you. If your husband knows that it's okay to pick up or caress his child when he feels like it, he will be more relaxed with her. He will see that there are no absolute rules that prevent his enjoying her. This allows him to give free rein to his spontaneity, enhancing not only his relationship with his child but also with you.

So if the baby is asleep when her father comes home from work, let him gently pick her up or at least touch or caress her. Perhaps she won't cry; perhaps she won't even wake up. And the angelic countenance of a sleeping baby has a dramatic impact on all those who come in contact with her. This is a unique opportunity for your husband to touch base with his baby, to sense the gentle quality of her skin, to touch the velvety softness of her hair, to feel her rhythmic breathing as he holds her gently in his arms. This is truly starting from the beginning, and you will feel a joy at contributing to your husband's fascination and evolving closeness with his child.

Try to provide a protective space for the family at this time. For example, put the newspaper and the mail out of sight, and tell anyone who phones that you're both busy at the moment and will call back later. Homecoming has been a very special time for me as a father. When I came in the door Claudia would say to Jonathan, "Look, Daddy's here!" And by two months Jonathan, perhaps in response to her enthusiasm, began greeting me with a grin that seemed large enough to swallow up the room. When that happened, Claudia would often comment, "Marty, see how much he loves you?" Coming home from work was a moment I looked forward to with eager anticipation.

In the beginning, any time your husband picks up the baby and she cries, he will be quick to see this as a rejection. He thinks, "See, she doesn't really like her father." It is up to you to say something hopeful and supportive like, "You're doing fine, honey," or "She cried when I held her this afternoon too," or "She'll calm down after a few minutes." And you might show him the position you held her in that soothed her cries. But however he's holding her, you can comment on how well he's doing it. Reinforce his sense of competence in every way you can. Sometimes merely feeling that he's not making a mess of things is enough. I remember the sense of relief I felt when Claudia first said, "That's okay, honey. Jonathan does that with me too." I suddenly realized it wasn't just me.

Your husband's playtime with the baby will be particularly significant, for playing sets his imaginative and creative aspects in motion. It encourages his spontaneity and lets him reach out to his child on her level. And if the baby smiles or coos or laughs with him, his pleasure is enhanced a hundredfold. His play then becomes more vital and more intense, for he has the promise of future responses from his baby. He feels that his child is responding uniquely to him, that she knows her father. A father, in playing, is focusing all of his resources and energy on his child.

Another important way to enhance your husband's relationship with the baby is to have him take walks with her in the baby carrier. If he seems reluctant to do this at first, then you carry her in it when you all take a walk together. Then you could ask him if he would like to try carrying her himself. Or if you grow tired, ask him if he would relieve you with her. For many husbands, this will be the first taste of prolonged close contact with the baby.

Once your husband has come to enjoy carrying the baby on walks with you, encourage him to try it without you, even though he may feel uncertain about how to handle an emergency if you're not there. What a father considers an emergency is usually an unrelenting howl that is unresponsive to his best efforts. The crying usually means that the baby is tired, hungry, wet, or soiled, and you can suggest that he simply bring her home to be taken care of. Later when he has a bit more confidence, he will begin to enjoy the walks so much he will probably just change her or feed her himself. I used to take a small amount of apple juice in a baby bottle to offer Jonathan when he became irritable. Most babies respond well to apple juice or other mild liquids, and it might help your husband to try this on his walks. He could also take an eight-ounce can of a ready-to-feed infant formula.

The important thing about the infant carrier is that this kind of leisurely, prolonged contact will both stimulate and recharge your husband's parenting battery.

♦ Primary Care

As your husband begins to feel more at ease with the baby, encourage him intermittently to take over her primary care. Initially this might be for only a few minutes each day, but as he becomes increasingly experienced, he could take over for longer periods.

Primary care time enhances a father's relationship with his infant in several ways. First, of course, it provides him with physical contact, which is the most important single ingredient in fortifying his link with his child. Second, his participation in basic care means that he is spending much more time with his child. (By the same token, if he does *not* participate in basic care, he is excluding himself from his child for significant amounts of time.)

Third, his being the one primarily responsible for the baby at that moment creates an emotionally powerful situation. Clearly there has been a space made for him. Now he is the one who is in charge. His infant's welfare rises and falls on his attentions. Caring for his infant seems to set a father's nurturing and protective instincts in motion.

They have been there all along but may not have been drawn upon unless there were times when you were actually unavailable to care for the baby. A father's awareness that at this moment the infant is completely dependent on him heightens the intensity of the experience and enhances his engrossment in his baby.

Perhaps you will find that it is not easy for you to encourage your husband to take over the care of the baby. You may be surprised at your resistance to giving her to him, and later, surprised at the rapidity with which you feel the need to "come to the rescue." Your husband's entry into your territory can create a sense of confusion and uncertainty as to your role. You may feel displaced. These feelings, which you might not be aware of, could cause you to give out negative cues to your husband, even though on the surface you want him to take over.

There is still another stumbling block to his caring for the baby. What will you do when she starts crying? Most mothers will instinctively run into the room and pick up the baby, even taking her out of her father's arms. This is usually a serious error. For how can a father learn to care for his child except by caring for her—without your racing in to rescue her?

Perhaps it will be difficult for you to see your husband having a tough time with tasks that you yourself have only recently mastered. His consternation and anxiety will probably trigger considerable anxiety in you. And when you hear your infant cry, you are likely to have an irresistible urge to grab her and take over. But somehow you will have to keep your rescue efforts in check. By consistently grabbing the baby away from your husband you reinforce the message to him, "You are inept and incompetent."

The impact of that not-so-subtle message may not only make him angry with you but also cause him to withdraw from further efforts at primary care. He feels like a bumbler. Naturally your husband may require some help from you with the baby at first. So how can you provide support and at the same time give the message that you have confidence that he can handle primary-care tasks without you?

I recommend a very simple approach: First demonstrate the procedure your husband is about to undertake—for example, giving the baby her feeding or her bath—then leave the room. Be sure your husband agrees to your leaving. He may want you to be more available at first, in case he needs help. Even though you may see yourself as rather inexperienced with infants, you probably have considerably more training than he has. Unless he grew up in a large family, it is quite possible that this is his first significant contact with a newborn baby.

If your husband is feeling unsure and anxious, point out to him that you were insecure and fearful yourself when you were alone with the baby for the first time. Let him know that you will be available if he needs your help. If he is still uncertain, you may have to stay around until the second or third time he feeds or bathes the baby. When you feel he is ready to try it on his own, however, go ahead and leave the room. Make yourself available by letting him know you'll be back in fifteen minutes to see if he needs any help.

A crucial principle to follow next is to get out of earshot! This provides you with a psychological buffer zone so that you can resist the need to carry out any immediate rescue operations. If the baby has been crying all day and you've been there with her, this will also give your shattered nerves an opportunity to recoup. The backyard is an excellent refuge, because you are close enough to respond to your husband's call for help yet far enough away to drown out any infant cries. Or go to a neighbor's home for a brief period. If the weather is too bad to go outdoors, simply go into the bedroom and close the door.

The important thing in all of this is for your husband to begin to develop his own sense of initiative with the baby. Let him get the feeling that you trust him with her and that you feel he has the skills to carry it off.

It is absolutely amazing how "being in charge" brings out the best in us. Suddenly your husband is aware of newfound dexterity. His previously stiffened fingers, neck, and arms begin to loosen. It is as if he had been crippled and has now found the cure: "primary-care responsibility." His brow, earlier wrinkled in a frown, loosens up, and a smile begins to light his face as he plays with his baby. The infant, sensing her father's ease and relaxation, begins to enjoy her bath and appears to experience the sensual pleasure of the warm water. Perhaps she stops crying. She smiles and coos and splashes about, showing her father how much she likes her bath. The halting of a child's crying is the absolute confirmation to the father that "At last my kid is not miserable in my presence." As infant and father together experience the pleasure of this activity, your husband will be increasingly more ready and eager to attempt the bath and other primary-care responsibilities the next time around.

♦ Time Alone: Strategies

When your husband is spending time alone with his baby, undertaking her primary care, he feels closer and more bound to her. He feels better about himself as well, more positive about his fathering role, more a part of the family. This seems to be true even of fathers who initially show little interest or enthusiasm in caring for their baby.

As long as you are present, however, the baby will tend to focus on you for the satisfaction of her needs. Your husband will tend to step aside to let "the expert" take over. So get out of the house, or get *them* out of the house, so father and child can have the opportunity to focus on each other.

Encourage your husband to take over with the baby by simply making an honest appeal to him. If you've been home all day with the baby, tell your husband you need some rest from the constant demands of child care. You need to get out of the house, or perhaps you just need some time to unwind in your own room. It's been a tough day and you're feeling exhausted, trapped. If you've worked at an outside job all day, you also need help with the baby. Sharing these feelings with him will help you to feel less burdened by the frustrations of child care. And sharing feelings is infinitely better than venting them angrily.

When you make this kind of appeal to your husband, it reverses his trend toward isolation and noninvolvement, his feeling of being displaced and unnecessary. You and the baby need him. Even though caring for the baby should ultimately become a pleasurable task for him, be prepared for some degree of protest at first. He will probably agree to taking over for a short time, but he may complain. You may feel, "But I want him to take care of his child because he wants to, not because I want him to." Don't panic. Remember that as he gains competence, his complaints will fade away.

Even though I said earlier that the father's arrival home from work can be an important time for contact with his baby, this is not true for all fathers. Some men feel too preoccupied or fatigued to respond at this time. One young father told me, "When I get home I just want to relax. Sometimes I'll even find myself reading the classified ads of all things, which helps me to unwind." Another father, fearful that he would be hit with many demands before he was ready on his arrival home, would park in the Safeway parking lot and read his newspaper for about twenty minutes before going home. Many men need help in moving past the stultifying aspects of their adult work world and shifting their mental and emotional gears. Give your husband a chance to relax if he needs it. If you talk to him, focus on the positive aspects of the day, whether it be about your job or the day at home. If you've been with the baby, talk mostly about the fun and enjoyable times. It is important that you be able to share the frustrations of the day with your husband also, but don't allow that to be your primary focus at homecoming. After fifteen or twenty minutes of rest, reading, or conversing, your husband may have shifted gears enough to feel like spending some time with his infant.

If your husband regularly arrives home from work before you do, perhaps he can be the one to provide some protected space before you take over with the baby. Or perhaps the baby's day caretaker can provide it for you both.

Resist any temptation to demand rather than request that your husband care for the baby. It makes a world of difference, because he needs to view his contact with her as voluntary, not something he is forced to do. The resentment associated with a demand makes it harder for him to respond to the baby and may make his time alone with her seem like a chore. But your reaching out to him in an affirmative way will have a positive impact on him. It is this atmosphere of sharing with and caring for each other that enhances the vibrant energy of the marital relationship. And what an eyeful it is to see a father doting on his little baby! This will be a unique reward for all your efforts.

The realization that the man at your side is capable, interested, and involved in his child also takes some of the pressure off you. Even though you may still spend much more total time with your infant than your husband does, the knowledge that he can competently take over in a pinch and even enjoys doing so, eases tremendously the feeling of being trapped. This allows you to enjoy to a greater degree your own contacts with your baby. In this way your patient encouragement, support, and understanding in helping your husband establish contact with his newborn will inevitably reap benefits for the entire family.

♦ Summary

Below is an outline of some simple guidelines that may help you in reaching out to your husband to help him hook up with your baby. Most of them are things we have talked about in this chapter.

Here are some important *don'ts.*

Don't belittle your husband's ability or his concerns about being a good father. Don't grab the baby away from him. Don't ever refuse to let him hold the baby because you're feeling angry or irritable with him. Don't oblige him to take care of the baby because you're angry with him. Don't ever talk to the baby about angry feelings toward your husband.

Don't undercut him. Don't make fun of him. Don't attack his insecurity. Don't carp. Don't do as you would not like to have done unto you by hospital staff, your mother, your mother-in-law. In this regard, do not use guilt as a weapon. For example, suppose your husband is with the child while you're out. If you come home and find your child with a runny nose, probably coming down with a cold, don't blame your husband. It's essential that you acknowledge whatever guilt you may feel for leaving the baby.

On the other hand, here are some important *do's.*

Do be understanding. Do be patient. Do compliment. Do encourage. Do try to keep your sense of humor and ability to laugh at yourself. Do attempt to point out those obvious positive aspects of the bond between your husband and the baby. Do attempt to make him aware of exciting changes as the baby grows and develops. Point out the unique ways in which the child looks like him. Indicate how good you feel about him in his involvement with the baby. Encourage him to play with her, to hold her and smile at her, to fondle and cuddle her. Encourage him to talk and sing to her, and even to dance with her. Encourage him to have a special song to sing to her. Encourage him to participate in the baby's visits to the doctor with you. Encourage him to take walks with the baby. Emphasize how important his care of her is to you, how it gives you not only relief but much pleasure to see him enjoying her.

Remember that in encouraging your husband to care for the baby, you are like a teacher. This requires a great deal of energy, patience, and resourcefulness, as well as the crucial ingredient of humor.

·18·

Spelling: Providing Relief in Child Care

There is no question about the stress of child care. The stress increases significantly with each additional child, and it reaches its peak when a mother feels isolated, without help from husband, friends, or family.

When sources of relief are absent, child care can become meaningless drudgery to your wife. She can become so locked in by her exhaustion that she loses sight of the uniqueness and wonder of her little boy. She may become irritable, tense, and quick-tempered, and find little pleasure in contact with him. Her mothering feels increasingly joyless and out of kilter.

The first months are a crucial period, in terms of how your wife views herself as a mother. The early feelings of sadness that are part of the post-partum blues may lower her frustration threshold and her ability to cope.[1] If she is also particularly hard on herself and demands perfection, she may overreact to difficulties with the baby and interpret his crying or fretfulness to mean that she is a bad mother. In this early period it's hard to imagine a more damaging accusation. Feeling that she must do everything well—cook, clean, take care of the new baby, be a good wife—she may finally be overwhelmed with all these demands.

Your role at such a time can be crucial. It is in these pressured circumstances that you can provide the help that may save the day. You can take over with the baby and let your wife lie down, get out of the house, or just get on with other work she needs to do, momentarily freed from child care. I call this relief *spelling.*

When I talk about spelling, I generally do so in terms of husbands spelling their wives, since in most families, even when women are working, it is still the mother who takes the primary responsibility for the child. But remember that there may be times when you are alone with the baby and need to be spelled by your wife. So it is a principle that applies to both parents.

♦ Difficulty in Accepting Relief

In spelling your wife with the baby, you must be able to tune in to when she is having problems with him. There may be times, however, when despite her clear need for relief, your wife is reluctant to let you take over. And you may experience similar situations yourself.

Why is it so hard for new parents to admit, "I need help"? Perhaps it is because accepting help seems like admitting failure. Spelling your wife is like a starting pitcher receiving relief from the bull pen in a baseball game. Despite the fact that the starting pitcher doesn't have his usual stuff, that his fastball has lost its customary zing, that his curveball has lost some of its snap, he leaves the game with reluctance If he had his choice he would stay in there pitching despite his continued ineffectiveness. It is as if he has become locked into the situation and lost his sense of perspective.

Continuing in a situation where they are increasingly exhausted, irritable, and impatient is counterproductive for parents as well as for the baby. It is ironic that it is often the parent who needs relief most urgently who most vehemently protests againt it.

♦ Establishing Spelling Guidelines

Because of this difficulty in accepting help, and the general potential for misunderstandings among most new parents, it is crucial that some guidelines for spelling be drawn up. Here are some suggestions:

1. Discuss the overall issue of spelling beforehand, at a time when neither of you feels threatened. In this way you can gradually develop the mutual acknowledgment that each of you may require relief at some time or another.

2. Spelling should be nonjudgmental. This means it should occur without critical comments or putdowns, such as "Can't you do anything right?"

3. Spelling should not linger on the difficulties the caretaking parent is experiencing. Rather, it should be smooth, rapid, and matter-of-fact.

4. Work out your signaling system in advance. A nonverbal cue such as the raising of the pinkie finger could indicate, "It's time for me to take over." It is a reminder that says, "Remember what we talked about before? You're getting into trouble. I think you need help." Yet it's not verbalized. This allows the parent who is being relieved the opportunity to initiate talking about the difficulty.

This flexibility of choice is essential. To your wife your verbal comments, even when made in the most neutral fashion, can sound like a criticism of her mothering ability and result in an angry response. She is already angry and critical of herself. Those continued shrieks of the baby, despite her best efforts, result in an increase in her self-doubts, and with this comes a vulnerability to feeling criticized.

♦ Facing the "Great Mother" Expectation

Your wife's turmoil about her mothering role reflects a current confusion in our culture. For a long time spelling went against our grain. We could not accept the fact that mothers needed relief. The good mother was all-loving, all-knowing, and all-powerful, able to do everything that needed doing for her children. This is the archetype of the "great mother," an image so powerful it is worshipped as a deity in many cultures.[2] In this image of mother we could not recognize her struggles—her anxieties, disappointments, angers, exhaustions. To acknowledge these would be to recognize that she is only human.

The image of your wife as an "imperfect" mother may not be easy for you to accept. The idea of the great mother is very appealing. It reminds us of when we were children and our mothers cared for us. Of course our image of our mothers is distorted by time and our needs. But if you remember your own mother as loving, always there when you wanted or needed her, you may want to perpetuate that all-caring image. If you remember her as never or rarely there when you needed her, you may have been searching for some time to find a replacement. With your wife's emergence now as a mother, there is an increasing tendency to elevate her to the position of the great mother.

Of course, this image has gradually been changing as it has clashed with the realities of today's world. Mothers increasingly work out of the need to help support their families and the desire for personal achievement and gratification. Still, it is difficult for many women to see the image of the great mother stripped from them. Working mothers often feel deep regret at not being able to fulfill it, and when home with their children they may be driven by guilt to make things up to them.

Perhaps your wife is eager to accept her crown of the great mother. For its image throws out a light that catches many in its radiant glow. It's nice to be wanted and needed. The woman then knows what is expected of her: everything. And many women leap to become ever available and ever competent, never asking for help. But it is a role that although initially gratifying can become increasingly suffocating. For it does not recognize her uniqueness, her creativity, or her humanity.

Often without realizing it your wife places the crown of the great mother on her own head. Perhaps it is an ancestral crown passed to her by her mother, who was given it by *her* mother, and so on up and down the line. And your wife's mother, as an affirmation of her own life strivings, expects her daughter to do likewise. No wonder your wife feels trapped, bound to do what is expected of her. So in order for you to offer her a helping hand, and for her to accept, you may both first have to clash head-on with your great-mother expectations.

Talking about these expectations is essential. And as you do, each of you will begin to see their rootedness in the past. More important, as a husband you will begin to understand your wife's unreasonable expectations of herself. You will hear it in her doubts about her performance as a mother as well as in her concern about what her friends, neighbors, and other family members think of her. She especially worries about what you think of her as a mother.

♦ The Psychological Toll

But what's wrong with your wife's being the great mother, with being all things to her children, with being always available, with not needing help? Can't she find happiness in this role? Perhaps. But at what cost?

All too many women, not only mothers of today's generation but also those of twenty and thirty years ago, have shared with me a sense of being overwhelmed and devoid of feelings, just going through the motions like automatons, when faced with the stresses of raising a new baby. They felt alone and isolated. Their uncertainty, anxiety, and depression at times reached such heights that they felt like they "might go crazy." They felt unable to ask their husbands for help because "it just wasn't done—you were supposed to make it on your own." And the husbands, unaware of their wives' struggles, rarely offered a hand. Some of the women sought counseling or psychotherapy to help them deal with their chaos.

What surprised me was that many of these women appeared so basically capable and self-confident. How could raising a baby have ravaged even these adequate and able women? Is it that tough? Perhaps we fathers can begin to understand the answers to some of these questions if we take a closer look at what these women are experiencing. If they could speak in one voice, this is what they might say:

> "There seems to be no limit in terms of the amount of time and energy that you can spend taking care of that baby. And it doesn't seem to matter whether you are available twelve hours or twenty-four. Your child is like a sponge that sucks up everything you can give. You feel overwhelmed with constant demands: the crying, the dirty diapers, the getting up in the middle of the night. You feel exhausted, without energy. Who could even think about sex, let alone enjoy it, in such circumstances? You feel barely able to survive. There is never an end in sight, no sign of relief from the demands of the child and the household work. You feel trapped in a situation without hope of escape. At times you feel enraged, but you hold it in. Sometimes you just feel like screaming."

♦ Nurturing Your Wife

Your wife may be feeling very alone and deserted. Images of having been alone in her childhood may come to her mind, further heightening her feelings. So where does a woman turn for help, even for short-term relief? The baby's grandparents may be unavailable. Friends, more often than not, have their hands full with their own families. A psychotherapist might provide emotional help, but perhaps there are no funds available. Or your wife may reject the possibility, saying, "I'm not crazy. I can do it myself."

You are the one person who can provide sustained support on a continuing basis. You do this by being sensitive to her needs and by withholding your critical judgments. You nurture her by showing increased patience and a willingness to take over some of the household tasks. And you nurture by empathizing with her and communicating your understanding as she describes her anxieties and uncertainties about taking care of the new baby. Some of her struggles may seem unimportant, or even unnecessary to you. But for the new mother, each and every question and concern involving the newborn baby assumes major proportions, as perhaps they should.

Not only does spelling provide time for your wife to rest, it helps her to gain perspective so that she can regroup to face the infant once again. It helps her to recharge her parenting battery. She can then return, refreshed and renewed, able to respond to the baby with greater flexibility and spontaneity. And most important, by breaking the vicious chain of fatigue, frustration, and anger that can feed back to the child in a destructive fashion, she can now experience delight and joy in contact with the baby.

♦ Anger—Fear of Losing Control

The experience of continuing frustration and anger toward the baby without an opportunity for relief is a potentially explosive situation.[3] Ignoring the anger results only in its gathering more energy and power. And since negative feelings toward the baby are extremely difficult to acknowledge, the situation can become an impasse.

When the anger has been fully felt, most new parents, mothers and fathers alike, are filled with guilt and fear. Their fear is that they could have lost control and impulsively struck out at their child. They think, "Oh, my God, I felt enraged! How could that happen! What if I lost control? Oh no, not me. I'd never dream of hurting my baby. It's not possible, not me!"

In our mind's eye, our angry feelings are indistinguishable from angry actions and being out of control. This possibility is so frightening that we must hide it from ourselves. But giving our anger and our fear the light of day—talking about them—tends to decrease their power.

♦ Spelling and Anger

The more involved you become with your baby, the greater will be your own need for spelling from your wife. And as you participate more with your baby, you begin to intuitively sense those situations when your wife will most need your help. For you know which situations are most difficult for you, times when you have hoped and prayed that your wife would finally walk in the door. And home alone with the baby, you also realize how frightening it can be to be in a situation where you feel angry and fear that you might lose control.

Such a situation happened to me. Claudia had gone to a class and I was home caring for six-month-old Jonathan. He woke up from a nap crying fiercely at about six o'clock in the evening. Usually when this happened I was able to soothe him. But this time he not only didn't respond to me but began crying more. I offered him a bottle, but he acted as if I had insulted him and threw it down. I stroked his head, which often calmed him, but his crying only became more piercing. So I placed him on my shoulder and tried patting his back gently. As I stroked him, I felt a sharp twinge of pain on the side of my neck. Jonathan had bitten me!

I was suddenly filled with rage. I felt a powerful impulse to strike back at him, and it was all I could do to resist it. I sat him down on the bed abruptly and said sharply and angrily, "Jonathan, you don't do that." At this, he began to cry louder and with greater intensity. It was at this point that I realized how angry I felt, and it frightened me. I thought, "My God, I felt like hitting him, smashing him! I could have lost control!" My guilt was nearly overwhelming. "I almost lost my head. I could have done anything!" I felt an incredible sense of anger at myself, along with a feeling of humiliation. At that moment I was not able to distinguish *feeling* out of control from *being* out of control.

I had to gain redemption for my sin. If only Jonathan would forgive me! But the only way he could show he forgave me was to stop crying.

I started carrying him through the house in the football position. It was like a marathon course: around the dining-room table, into the kitchen, back to the living room, through the hallway into our bedroom, across to Jonathan's bedroom, and then down the hallway, and I started through the course again and again and again. Every time I stopped, he began sobbing again, and my guilt would egg me on to further effort. I carried him in this frantic fashion for two and a half hours.

I must have been quite a sight as I relentlessly pursued the course through the house. But for me it was deadly serious business. I was filled with tension: My stomach was all knotted up, there was a tight band across my forehead, and I was on the verge of tears.

As I walked, I desperately wished Claudia would come home, to take me off the hook. I needed her to give me some relief. I felt like a total failure. When she finally arrived and found me carrying Jonathan through the house, she asked, "What in the world are you doing?"

"Oh, Jonathan is kind of tense and irritable," I said, "and every time I stop he wakes up." I still felt ashamed, humiliated, and extremely guilty, and I was unable to share what had happened with her.

Frankly, until that time I had been so immersed in my son's attractive attributes that I hadn't stopped to look at much else. I had been busily writing and thinking about fathering, but mostly its positive aspects. I hadn't bothered to look at some of the more painful issues parents face.

I was so upset about those events that I never recorded them, as I did many of the other day-to-day occurrences with Jonathan. It was only later as I described this night at a conference about children that many participants urged me to have the courage to share the experience. They pointed out that coping with anger was the other side, and acknowledging only the joyful aspects of the child neglected the reality struggles, the frustration, and the anger that so many parents face.

Later, as I talked with more and more parents, I began to realize that coping with anger and the fear of losing control is a universal struggle among all new parents. One of the problems in this particular struggle is that once we realize that our feelings have been "contaminated" by anger, we no longer trust them. We must deny our feelings. And the cost is high, for in the process we lose touch with ourselves. We limit our feelings with one prohibition after another. We cannot show anger. We cannot ask for help. We cannot reveal our imperfections. To do so invites ultimate punishment and humiliation before the world. In such a situation it is no wonder some parents experience difficulty in getting in touch with the joys of parenthood.

♦ Spelling: Defusing the Anger

Spelling helps us break out of this destructive cycle. For the knowledge that a spouse is available, concerned, and willing to provide relief and support is extremely important in helping one cope. Anger on a steady basis leads to overwhelming guilt and diminished self-esteem. And it increases the likelihood of a parent's actually breaking loose in a physical attack on the child. Furthermore, the more frustrated and tense we feel, the more difficult child care becomes. We have less patience, energy, and resourcefulness to contend with situations we might otherwise have handled with ease.

♦ Acute Father Emergency (AFE)

The necessity for relief can at times reach emergency proportions. If you don't make an extra effort to help your wife then, you'll pay it later when the eruption occurs.

Claudia and I call this crisis situation an Acute Father Emergency, or AFE. You can assume that an AFE is approaching if your baby has been crying without letup and is unresponsive to all of your wife's efforts. Or perhaps your wife's voice is becoming increasingly tense and shrill or her anger toward the baby seems to be building. If she hasn't had much sleep lately and has been perpetually exhausted, the baby's cries may trigger an AFE much earlier than when she is well rested.

The situation reaches emergency proportions when your wife begins to feel out of control. This can be expressed as feeling increasingly frustrated or irritable, feeling like she's going to explode, feeling like she can't take it any longer. She badly needs to escape for a while. And in this kind of situation the infant's crying usually escalates, increasing her feelings of frustration and failure.

I remember a typical AFE when Jonathan was about two months old. He had been crying continuously, and Claudia begged me to get him out of the house. So I took him for a walk, during which he quieted down. But when I brought him back home, he began crying again. And my wife again appealed for protection from his crying, saying she couldn't take it any longer. This went on continuously throughout the day. By the time I had taken him on his eighth walk, I too felt completely exhausted. But by this time Claudia was well rested and able to take over without difficulty.

♦ Competition

As parents begin to share child-care responsibilities and spell each other in time of need, another area of conflict can emerge; namely, competition. Competition in and of itself is not destructive. There's nothing wrong with wanting to be as effective as your wife with the baby, to be able to hold him or bathe him or feed him with ease and comfort. Competition only becomes destructive when you begin to view parenting as a contest and actually hope your mate will fail. This sentiment is bound to have negative repercussions.

Of course some degree of competition is inevitable. Both of you are trying to be "good parents," and the failure of one parent can to some degree reflect the success of the other. As a very benign example of this, one father commented to me about his three-month-old baby:

> "Whenever the baby is getting more and more fussy and I see my wife getting more irritable and upset I take over. I notice then that the baby is unusually responsive to me, as if he needed the relief too."

But competition must be minimized if spelling is to be effective. In the example above, the wife was delighted to be spelled by her husband when the baby was fussy. She even complimented him on his abilities. But what if she were insecure about her own abilities as a mother? She could easily have resented her husband's coping well when she was having difficulty. Talking about his successes could have been like rubbing salt in an open wound. Then, when he experienced difficulty she might have pointed out his own inadequacies.

This kind of situation can rapidly deteriorate into a contest between the husband and wife, and spelling then becomes increasingly difficult. The parent being relieved may feel she is not being given a real chance to succeed. Instead of feeling supported, she feels criticized. The offer to spell her is seen as a putdown.

Competition is most likely to arise after the first few months, as the baby's behavior becomes more complicated and more responsive to the external environment, including his parents. A temporary lack of response to you or your wife may then be seen as a disappointment, even a rejection. And the "rejected" spouse can easily become angry at the other, who appears to be succeeding.

As with so many problem areas, improved communication will help you cope with competition and keep it under control. By sharing your feelings, you are working together rather than against each other. And it is important that both of you feel good about yourselves as parents so that neither feels threatened by the other's successes. If you know you're a capable father, you're not going to be concerned with your wife's offer to soothe the baby, or vice versa.

♦ Inflation

At first, any success you have with your newborn may be an unexpected surprise. But as you become more capable with him, you may begin to anticipate your successes. It gets to the point where you have a hard time recognizing when you need help. At this point, inflation has begun to set in. And then watch out! For inflation can be as destructive as insecurity.

My own struggles with inflation were always short-lived. For example, when Jonathan was three months old we started giving him cereal. Claudia managed to get it down, but my attempts to feed him ended in failure, as he kicked and thrashed about unhappily. I developed a theory that the way to keep him from raising a ruckus was to keep the cereal coming fast, and on the first trial it seemed to work. I shoveled spoonful after spoonful into his mouth, giving him little opportunity to fuss. Afterward I bragged to Claudia that I had finished feeding Jonathan in ten minutes. She was amazed, as it usually took her a good thirty minutes. Still tooting my horn, I picked Jonathan up and placed him on my shoulder. With a loud, resounding burp he released every last spoonful of cereal he had just taken in.

My smile froze. I glanced at myself in the mirror. The cereal was now matted in my hair, my beard, and all over my chest. I was a mess. Claudia was rapidly tapping her foot, a scowl on her face. I felt like slithering out of the room. I had become so preoccupied with my own performance as a father and in competing with my wife that I had forgotten about Jonathan. I had been responding to my needs, not his. And my inflated view of myself had prevented me from asking for help in feeding him.

If you begin to see yourself as all-knowing, all-capable, and all-competent, beware of trying to uphold that image. It cuts you off from asking for help when you need it. Your interactions with your child become less spontaneous and vital, and more pressured and frantic. It's a do-or-die situation. A father who has gotten himself into this trap desperately needs help from his wife. You must learn to admit that there are times when you are in trouble, when you can do nothing right, when you need to back off from your child. No parent can do it all, and trying to do so will run down your parenting battery sooner or later.

You and your wife need to develop a sense of yourselves as having both capabilities and shortcomings. Then when you spell each other not only is it a sharing but it also adds to each other's sense of self, both as a parent and as a human being.

•19•

Who Changes the Diapers?

It is particularly important for you and your wife to make some basic agreements in terms of contact and care of the newborn. These agreements should always be made during a lull on the child-care battleground, either when your little boy is asleep or when you and your wife are having an evening free together, without the baby. Free time together allows the two of you some breathing time and is a good time for making agreements without haste or anger.

One crucial agreement would be that if you pick up your baby when he is quiet or sleeping and he starts howling, you will take the responsibility of dealing with the situation rather than dropping him into your wife's lap with a "Here, you take care of him, he's beginning to cry." If your wife knows in advance that you will at least try to quiet the baby, it will allay any apprehension she might feel when you pick him up.

Would you believe that making an agreement about diaper changing may be one of the greatest challenges you will face in those early months? Acrimonious debates may await the couple who avoid this problem area. In some families it is still the woman who is called upon to change the diapers. When the father is playing with his child, he may notice that the infant is wet or soiled. Then comes the inevitable, "Honey, he needs his diapers changed." But if a father is going to enjoy the pleasures of cuddling and playing with his baby, it makes sense for him to reap those byproducts that come with that activity. It is extremely frustrating to a woman to reap all of the negative fruits of the baby while her husband enjoys only the positive fruits.

When, in fact, you start to participate in changing your baby's diapers, you'll probably find that it's not such a big deal after all. For example, a father commented:

"Changing the diapers was easy. I got it down to thirty seconds. We always used disposable diapers, so that part was simple. I was prepared for trauma. Maybe it's because I was expecting something bad that it was so easy. I was thinking it would take probably ten minutes each time to clean him up and wash him and put on medication. So I guess I was prepared for a lot, but it seems like it doesn't take that much."

In the days before disposable diapers, there was an uninviting aura about the whole subject of diapers. Cloth diapers might frequently be found rinsing in the toilet, and laundering them was such a prodigious task that diaper service became a flourishing business. But nowadays, disposable diapers are available to virtually all parents and accepted by nearly all pediatricians. This has revolutionalized child care. You simply dispose of the diaper and have no concerns about rinsing, laundering, drying, folding, and putting them away.

Disposable diapers have also made it much easier to travel with your baby, since you don't have to worry about where to keep the dirty ones. And even if you run out of diapers while away from home, you can almost always find another parent who will donate a diaper or two to help your cause. For there is a close bond among all parents, an empathy born of common struggles.

It is difficult to find a course or book on child-raising with an honest discussion of diapers and diaper changing, particularly of the more challenging emotional aspects and its potential for marital infighting. It's a subject that is often passed over lightly. But despite this, babies continue to go about their own business, and the frequent emptying of their bowels and bladders is a way of life for them as well as a sign of their continuing good health and development.

The fact is that mothers and fathers not only spend a great deal of time talking about diapers and their contents, but also about their reluctance to face these contents. Every couple has their own shorthand term for these products. Urine is variously referred to as wet diaper, pee or peepee, number one, tinkle, tee or teetee, sis or sissy, wee or weewee. And bowel movements have an even greater variety of names, including soiled diaper, dirty diaper, dirty didies, kaka, deedee, dump, number two, stool, BM, doodoo, doody, poo, and poopoo. Then there are the designations hush-hushed by the experts yet often used by parents, particularly when they're feeling frustrated and angry about the diaper contents.

With Jonathan, Claudia and I used the terms peepee and poopoo, and these are the ones I will use in this chapter. These words tend not to have a derogatory ring. And you can feel fairly comfortable about using them with your infant as he grows and develops. This is not true of some of the earthier terms, which might result in your being red-faced if your child later blurts them out in front of your guests (although you'll probably chuckle a bit too).

Then too, your use of terms that are not disparaging will allow your infant to refer to excretions comfortably, accepting them and therefore himself more readily. If your wife insists that changing the diapers is her role and your expectations mesh with hers, there will be little debate as to who changes the diapers. However, women increasingly expect their husbands to participate in diaper changing as part of the shared care of the baby. Not only this, but they recognize that the father's refusal to do so will result in an increased distance from the baby. One mother commented:

> "You hear a lot of men say, 'I'll do everything else, but I'm not going to change the diapers. That's where I draw the line.' But that's so much a part of having a baby. And that's so much a part of the time that you spend with the baby. I mean, you change diapers eight or ten times a day—if you don't ever do that, you're missing a lot of minutes with that baby."

If the mother further sees her husband's refusal to change diapers as a rejection of the baby, she can become extremely unhappy with him about that, as well as about his failure to help her out with one of her less desirable tasks.

♦ Finders Keepers

The issue of diaper changing can seem like a deadly serious business unless you let yourself relax about it and accept the inevitable. After all, contact and involvement with your child are bound to mean taking over aspects of his care. If you spend all day with your child you need to know how to feed him and how to change his diapers. These are just activities that go with the turf. And changing a diaper is a small price to pay for the opportunity for increased closeness with your baby. Knowing how to take care of your child becomes essential if your wife is away or ill or working, while you're at home. You do what you have to, to care for him. There is little or no conflict in these circumstances.

There are a number of gray-zone situations, however, that can trigger tension and anger between parents. Basically, here is the issue: Most fathers won't resent changing a wet diaper or two. It's the soiled diapers—the poopoo diapers—that trigger the discussion, grumbling, and discontent. If your wife is home with the baby during the day she may hope, anticipate, and expect that you will change the diapers when you are home, regardless of the contents. After all, she has quite literally had her hands full of diapers all day long. But you may reason, why should you change the baby when he's with her more than he's with you? Why should your wife have this loving, positive relationship with him, and when you get home all you get is the dirty diapers? You may grumble and protest, and your wife is likely to be annoyed with you, even if you do finally change him.

One solution, of course, is to make an agreement that the person who is with the baby at any moment in time, who notices a wet or soiled diaper, is the person who should change him. This is the course of action followed by many couples. However, there is a key word here: "notices." There are all levels of observation, and it can be amazing how the poopoo diapers fail to be noticed. It is here that stealth comes into play and fathers as well as mothers can be guilty of this.

What if you suspect that the baby has a poopoo diaper but you don't confirm it? Suppose, at that moment of suspicion, you busy yourself with something else. Perhaps you hear a familiar noise, catch a whiff of a potent odor as you approach his door and tell yourself, "I'd better water the lawn or clean out the garage." You didn't really notice the poopoo diaper, so you can't really be accused of having known—you only suspected and you could have been wrong! Right?? So you leave, hoping your wife will discover the diaper and change him. "Finders keepers. What she finds, she gets."

Well, this amusing situation, though hilarious in retrospect, can lead to increasing discontent. Stealth by one partner leads to stealth by the other, and you may discover to your chagrin that two can play this game of nondiscovery. Perhaps your wife will busy herself in the kitchen at a time when she knows that the baby usually has a soiled diaper, allowing you to discover it.

Another potential scenario is this. Your wife notes how efficient you are at changing diapers. You probably don't like it any better than she does, but perhaps you change them without noisy protest. I myself was part of such a scenario. In wanting to care for my child, I undertook diaper changing with a minimum of grumbling. Besides, a deficit in my sense of smell allowed me to do it with more ease than Claudia.

However, I eventually began to notice a remarkable improvement in my smelling apparatus. This seemed to coincide with an increasing awareness that there were unusual numbers of poopoo diapers being bestowed upon me when I arrived home. Perhaps the large amount of practice had resulted in finely tuning my nostrils' capability. Finally I confronted my wife. "Claudia, are you saving Jonathan's poopoos for me?" I was half angry but half joking. The situation was deadly serious, but it was also rather amusing. Claudia laughed and confessed, "But, honey, you're so good at it."

So you can see that stealth needs to be faced and talked about. In many ways, you might argue, it's easier to go back to the old days when women did all the diaper changing. At least there were no arguments about it. My reply to you is, "Will you surrender every time there is difficulty? Would you stop being a father just because there are stresses involved?" I assure you that your marriage need not be torn asunder by angry debates about poopoo diapers. What you need is to work out some basic agreements about the problem.

♦ Diaper Patrol

There are a number of different solutions to sharing responsibilities with the dirty diapers. These depend on you and your wife's individual inclinations and the degree of involvement that you want with your infant, and also to some extent on the external demands on you—other children, your work, and other home chores such as meals, cleaning, or household repairs

Probably one of the most simple and straightforward arrangements is one suggested to me by a young father who jokingly said that couples should set a schedule of "diaper patrol." I like that idea. This is how diaper patrol works. The schedule will depend on how involved you are able or want to be. For example, if you want to be very involved in your child's care, and you want to share these responsibilities with your wife, then you could agree to change all the dirty diapers there are while you're at home. This means you'd be on diaper patrol from 6:00 P.M. to 6:00 A.M. or thereabouts. Any diapers wet or soiled during that time zone would be your responsibility. It's a good idea for your official duties to begin about a half hour after your arrival home, which not only gives you some breathing time but avoids the problem of soiled diapers being saved up for Daddy's arrival.

Another system might be to schedule diaper patrol on alternate days or for varying hours on a given day. You could set up alternating three- or four-hour shifts, or any schedule that you and your wife want. The main thing is to develop some consensus on the issue, which may require not only discussion but some compromises on both sides.

When you can talk about and resolve the question of who changes the poopoos, you'll be able to talk about many of the other highly charged issues involved in child care, such as who gets up in the middle of the night when the baby is crying, or who wakes early in the morning to care for him. So the question of who changes the diapers, when faced, is really an entreé into increased communication, sharing, and humor between you and your wife.

• The Whole Child

When you can respond to your child, and coo and sing to him with good spirits even as you change his diapers, your engrossment in him will have entered another plane, an area of basic acceptance—of accepting your total child. Many parents comment on this. They have discovered that the relationship with the baby is different, somehow stronger, when it includes all aspects of the child's care, when it includes more than just playing together. A new mother put it this way:

> "There's a different kind of connection that you make with someone you physically care for. It's a real connection when you attend to a baby's physical needs."

This comment is also echoed over and over again by numerous fathers, who often mention the sense of accomplishment and pride they feel at being able to care for their babies on their own.

As your engrossment and initial fascination with your newborn evolves into growing feelings of love, you will find yourself increasingly able to accept all of him, including his waste products. Inevitably, at some point, he will benevolently make you the recipient of these products, and you'll find yourself able to tolerate this as well as other trying aspects of your baby with greater ease. It is this acceptance, this linkage, that later allows you to stay up with him when he is ill, to carry him when he is hurt, to talk to him with gentle tenderness when he is in pain, and cuddle and snuggle him when he needs protection.

Your increasing acceptance of your child and your ability to laugh will help modulate the anger that parents so often experience in child care. There is then a greater tendency to act, to do whatever needs to be done. And nowhere is this willingness more needed in the first year or so than in certain diaper situations. Occasions arise that would try any of us.

In a meeting of a group of new fathers, one young man laughed as he described a situation that he and his wife had dealt with.

> "We went through a stage where we didn't use the elastic-leg diapers, and we used to have a situation that we called a 'meltdown.' He would wake up from his nap very quietly in his crib. And before we knew he was awake, he had it smeared all over the crib, all over himself, so when you reached down to get him you didn't know where to touch. It was like a challenge. 'Okay, Dad, this is it, where are you going to get me this time?' We both got sent to the showers. There was just no other thing to do; just go in the bathroom and strip down and jump in the shower, because when you touched him you got it all over you too. Boy, he had some great pieces of art; it really covered the wall! We called him Poopoo Picasso!"

The father said that at the time he felt overwhelmed, but he was willing to do what was needed, and he had the saving grace of humor:

> "You're just devastated by the situation and its *instant humor.* You can't take it too seriously or you wouldn't be able to do anything about it. The situation was so ridiculously absurd, just looking at it, that there was no easy way out, there was no point in getting mad about it. It was there and had to be dealt with."

"And there wasn't time to have a beer and think it over," chimed in another father in understanding acknowledgment. Coping with diapers is a unique initiation ritual into parenting. One father put it this way:

> "There is no denying that you are a father once you've begun to change your baby's dirty diapers. It's like an initiation. It's a negative experience all fathers have to go through. It's sort of a hell week, a rite of passage, that bonds all fathers together. It's a common experience that they can relate to and laugh over that nonfathers haven't had any experience with."

Fathers experience a camaraderie in being able to talk about their struggles during this early period. The anecdotes about dirty diapers are frequently shared in the kind of aura that exists in a tightly closed secret society. The men seem to recognize that the subject is semitaboo, and only those who are going through this phase—coping with a small baby—will understand and be able to laugh about it. Others might regard this laughter and discussion as silly or even repugnant.

Well, I say to you that you can take these discussions out from behind closed doors. It's okay to have diaper talk, to laugh about experiences you've had with your infant's peepees and poopoos. Later you will look back on this phase with many chuckles, which will help you to continue coping with new situations as they arise. Life is much easier this way.

♦ The Best Laid Plans

You must accept the fact that no matter what agreement you and your wife make in advance, there will still be times when you feel frustrated, enraged, and ready to explode if you get one more dirty diaper. I was confronted with such a situation. Jonathan was eight months old. We were returning from a long trip in our fully laden Volkswagen bug. The car was filled with suitcases, diapers, bottles, a stroller, a baby car seat, a high chair, and a variety of other baby equipment. There was barely room to move. I had been driving for four hours and was feeling tired, cramped, and extremely on edge. We stopped briefly and got ready to change Jonathan. Since Claudia was sitting in an awkward position, she asked me to change him. The dramatic moment came when I asked, "Is it peepee or poopoo?"

"Peepee," Claudia replied.

It's not that I refused to change the diapers depending on the contents, but I always liked to know what I was getting into. Well, without further ado, I opened Jonathan's diaper. My eyes widened as I noted a small, semihardened stool tumbling onto my lap and rolling around like a ball on a roulette wheel, finally depositing itself inside my favorite beige sweater, which was now slightly tinged with brown. For a moment I was shocked and said nothing. Then, recovering, I roared, "You said there were no poopoos!" Claudia, who had been following the movement of the brown pellet, tried to reply without swallowing her fist, which she had jammed into her mouth to stifle her laughter. This enraged me further and I screamed even more loudly, "YOU TOLD ME THERE WERE NO POOPOOS!" That did it, Claudia broke into loud, hearty guffaws. And the more she laughed, the madder I got.

"Dammit!" I exploded, glaring at her, "It's not funny. That's my favorite sweater." Frankly, I wasn't really as upset about my sweater as I was about this earthy deposit upon my person. "You did it on purpose!" I screamed.

"No, I didn't," she protested, but continued laughing harder than ever.

For the next thirty minutes I drove in silence, alternately glaring at the road and at my wife, until the ludicrousness of the situation finally hit me and I began laughing so hard that I had to pull off the road. Claudia chuckled loudly, saying, "Hon, you looked so funny with that poopoo in your lap," which only made me laugh more. Sensing the fun, Jonathan added his own coos to this cacophony of mirth. We hugged, and I was aware of an intense closeness that enveloped all three of us.

It is the tribulations of parenting, followed by laughter and then closeness, that have given me my belief that finding the humor in down-to-earth realities provides us with a portal toward enrichment and joy in those early years. What you might have seen as a failure in your efforts you now can see as simply a sharing of your humanness. It is as if having tripped and fallen, splat!. . . you suddenly see the world from a new vantage point and view the joy, spontaneity, and humor from this new vista.

• A Final Word

There is something deeply important that may happen in the course of changing your baby's diapers, as part of your agreement with your wife: Be alert, as you wipe your baby's behind, for he may look you in the eye. And you will feel the unique touch of his skin and the pleasure of gazing on his little naked body. The diaper changing was just an excuse, a reason for setting up this whole experience for you. For your child, it was a genuine need. He didn't like sitting in his wet and soiled diapers. But now that you're here you can gaze on him, and wonder of wonders when your eyes meet. This is it. This can be the beginning of a relationship. If you weren't hooked up at birth, this is a new opportunity to become so. And if you were hooked up, this is a further opportunity to enhance and perpetuate that early bond.

•20•

The Circle of Life

"All of a sudden you find out, my gosh, I've been living the life of a human. I've been living this thing that repeats itself and returns always—childhood and then parenthood—and I never really suspected. It's just an amorphous feeling of being, all of a sudden, not an alienated human of the twentieth century but being the very end point, the next-to-the-last link in this long chain of being, or being on the circle that's starting over again with a new child."

—Words of a father after the birth of his first child.

Watching your child's development during his first year is like walking through the valley of time. For as your child grows older, beginning first to sit, then crawl, to stand, and finally to take his first hesitant steps, these milestones in his development remind us that we also are growing older. This passage of time, and your child's continuing movement from one phase to the next, is reflected also in the changing of the seasons. The changing times of year are still the backdrop against which I remember my own son's development.

I was studying and traveling in Europe during Jonathan's first year. He was four and a half months old when we first arrived in Switzerland. He was just beginning to sit by himself. It was the dead of winter, and I took him for walks even in the extreme cold, rain, and snow. We bundled him up in a snowsuit, hat, and mittens, and only his face was barely visible. I would place him in the backpack and take off across the fields and into the nearby forest.

As winter passed into spring, Jonathan began crawling. The snow that was on the ground where we walked had given way to new sprouts of grass and wildflowers. And a little brook had now become a stream that threatened to overrun its borders. Intermittently, the sky would burst forth with buckets of rain. Usually Jonathan and I had plenty of warning when that occurred; dark clouds would begin rolling across the face of the sun. If the rain came down inordinately hard, we would race to an old café where we would wait out the worst of the storm. I would run through the forest, slipping and sloshing as Jonathan bounced on my back, giggling at the special ride he was getting.

During the spring, Jonathan began making increasing efforts to stand by himself. At this time we often visited friends who lived in the rolling Swiss farmlands. Mornings there were an especially wonderful time. While everyone else slumbered, Jonathan would wake, ready and eager for action as the roosters were just beginning to crow. I would quickly get him dressed, put him in the backpack, and take off with him as the sun was just coming up. Although I was still half asleep, there was something majestic about the peaceful silence that enveloped us, with the Alps towering above us in the distance.

By this time, Jonathan was interested in every new thing and would make efforts to touch and talk to animals and objects in his world. As we passed a pen filled with pigs, Jonathan would squeal with delight, almost in time to the grunts coming from the muddy enclosure below. Sometimes a cow crossed the road, and I would encourage Jonathan to touch it as I guided his hand. He would gently brush the cow's side, then let out a coo, along with a loud, shrill laugh as he rapidly withdrew his hand. Then he would once more gain the courage to explore the new sensation of this strange animal, who munched on the grass seemingly oblivious to Jonathan's explorations.

One of the things I loved about my son as we walked together during the seasons of his first year was his openness to everything around him. As I allowed myself to be caught up with his enthusiasm, I would feel myself open up to the new views and vistas about me. I looked at things with greater awareness, seeing increasing nuances. It seemed as if I saw, heard, and smelled so much more.

These impressions of Jonathan's first year will stay with me always, just as the changing of the seasons will be a backdrop for your own newborn's unfolding development. Barely sitting in one season he will move on to crawling and gradually standing with support by the next season. By the time he is eight or nine months old he may even say his first word, and you may swear that it sounds like "Dada." By this time, although there are still struggles ahead, the anxiety and uncertainty of the first few months have diminished considerably. There now seems to be a certain rhythm to your life and the days flow by more rapidly.

As the seasons of your child's first year continue, he will be making further efforts to stand alone. Perhaps he attempts a step only to fall crashing to the floor. But he is giving you increasing signals that he will soon be walking. There is no way to avoid the fact your child is growing older. His increasing weight as you carry him in your arms is a constant reminder of his evolving development, and a reminder of your own mortality. You may have felt this sense of aging when you became a father for the first time. But your child's rapid development makes you constantly aware of this process.

As your newborn approaches one year of age you'll experience feelings of pride and joy in your child's continuing development, in his growing independence and evolvement into his own unique person. He is increasingly beginning to explore the world around him, and you can experience his world with your own new sense of awareness. As he grows older your closeness can now take other forms—rolling the ball about together, running together, talking together. And you may also feel that he is responding to you more as the months go by.

But there is also a sense of loss, and perhaps a sense of sadness. For the first birthday, with your child's increasing ability to walk, symbolically marks the end of his ultimate dependence on you. And if you had the early experience of companionship, of walking together with your baby, the closeness that came as you carried your child on your back or in your arms, or cooed and played together, you may have a hard time letting go and saying good-bye to this first year.

Of course, there is no radical change on your child's first birthday. With each new stage in your child's development, there is rarely a sudden change, but an evolving. Perhaps you think you will stop carrying your child on your back when he is old enough to walk. But in fact you may continue carrying him in the backpack until he is about one and a half, or even older. Then you can walk a little bit together, and take him for rides on your bicycle. As early as nine months to one year, your child will probably enjoy your wrestling and gently roughhousing with him. By one and a half to two, you can begin to tell him stories and read books with him as well as play hide-and-go-seek together. He will continue to enjoy these activities in some form for the next six to eight years and even longer, although they will become more sophisticated and elaborate as he grows. At age two or three, and increasing gradually as he gets older, he may enjoy going off on walking excursions with you and you can share what you know about trees and rocks, squirrels, insects, fish, and other animals. Sometimes at the end of an outing when he is tired he'll ask you to carry him on your shoulders, or he'll fall asleep in your arms and you'll remember earlier times when you carried him as a baby. Throughout this time you'll see him beginning to develop into his own person, with his own interests and capabilities.

When your child is four he may ride on your bicycle less and less, as he first gets his own three-wheeler and finally moves toward riding his own bicycle at age six to eight. Then you can once again enjoy bike rides together, although now he is moving on his own power. And this increasingly becomes the theme throughout his development—moving on his own power.

As your youngster's development proceeds, if you are alive to it there will occasionally be some dramatic event that makes you aware of how unique and wonderful he is. For me, one such moment was when Jonathan at ten months smiled and cooed and excitedly flapped his hands up and down when I asked him if he wanted to take a walk with me. And again when, at two and a half years, he said spontaneously, "I love you, Daddy." When he was four he dressed up in Indian bells and headdress and chanted and danced an American Indian dance that was so captivating I felt transported into a world of dreams and magic.

There is almost an irony in the intensity of your early experiences and your difficulties in letting go. Perhaps you remember how just a short time ago you were uncertain about the idea of a baby, your concerns about giving up your carefree days of freedom, and your fears and anxieties about becoming a father. And now here you are, so engrossed in your newborn child, so thoroughly enjoying your companionship together, that you may actually be feeling a tinge of sadness at his first birthday. How the wheel turns.

I've spoken before about the struggles with letting go. They are an important aspect of the parenting process and can start very early in the first year. This struggle was made evident to me in a chance meeting with a new mother when Jonathan was two months old. I was walking on the beach carrying him in the baby sling when I passed a young mother holding an eight-month-old baby. When she saw Jonathan she stopped to admire him and said, "Gosh, they're so cute when they're little. They grow up so fast. I wish mine was that small. Can I hold him?" I was amazed at the time, for it seemed to me that her eight-month-old baby was still plenty small.

My own struggles with letting go surfaced only a few weeks later. Jonathan was three months old and had grown so large that we had to take him out of his cradle and place him in a crib. I felt excited by his development, which was accompanied by his growing responsiveness. But I also felt some sadness, and I recognized that there was actually a part of me that would have liked to keep him little forever. This struggle with letting go is seen in a new father's response to his son's approaching first birthday. He commented:

> "My immediate reaction is that I don't like him getting older. On the other hand I am very excited that he is about to walk on his own. He is leaning, standing, moving, and he will be walking soon. That will be the next step, to be walking together. Everything has its place and time. . . ."

Changes in your child's development will result in changes in your relationship with him. His new achievements and abilities force you to let go, and there is a sense of loss. Then there is a moving on to a new phase and a coming together at a different level once again. Your experience of sadness and loss, and at the same time your joy in seeing your child's evolution, is a repetitive theme throughout his development. It is a part of the circle of life. We cannot hold life in one place. It moves on, constantly changing and growing. Experiences of the past add richness and zest to the present. And in doing so they form an everlasting circle—a constant wheel of life, or circle of return. We begin to see themes repeated throughout our own lives and we feel both happiness and sadness as we move on to different phases. Our ability to face our child's different stages allows him to move on, to get in touch with the potential within himself, to face the joy and fascination of the life process, and to live out his own cycle.

The realization that your child is growing older triggers more wonderings about the future. How will he develop? Will he be happy and enjoy life? Will he do well in school? Will you continue to be close and have a good relationship together? As you think about what the world will be like in later years after you are gone, you realize that your child is a part of your connection to the future, a link in the cycle of life. As a new father said to me:

> "My grandma used to watch horses and buggies, and now here is a guy on the moon. What is my daughter's generation going to see? The same thing I see, until she is grown up and married. And after I die she is going to see even more. It is kind of hard to judge what is going to happen—all the nuclear worries! We are the generation to change it—to keep the cycle of life going. I hope things just go on forever and ever. I hope my child's children will go on. And her children's children, and their children's children and so on. I hope it keeps going."

The realization that your child is growing older makes you aware that he is going to separate from you some day. You may experience some sadness as you visualize him already grown up. Here is one first-time father's reflections about his eleven-month-old daughter:

> "Periodically I wonder what it's going to be like when she is eighteen. It's going to happen so fast. From the beginning she wants to be close, but then she wants to separate and be out on her own. And that's what it's all about . . . giving up carrying her in my arms, facing her getting married, the separation! Accepting the way of things! Sad when I think about it. But you don't think about it, you think about it for a moment and then you go on. It is like something really good and close, and it is leaving. You have to accept the end and move on."

The symbolism of this time is that of life and death. Somebody is born and somebody dies. We have all seen this in our own lives. If you have experienced the death of a loved one, you may have greater difficulty in letting go of each stage in your child's development. For the end of each stage triggers memories of other endings, of which death is the ultimate one. And thus you may experience a double loss.

Birth and death themselves are not so far apart as we might be led to believe. During labor, some women feel that as they are giving birth, they experience an existential awareness of being close to death and are yet not fearful of it. This closeness is, of course, a psychological one, for a death in childbirth is a rare occurrence. Perhaps the feeling reflects the sense of oneness with the universe that some women experience as they give birth, a feeling of continuity with the life force, of which life and death are a part.

One woman described the moment of birth of her second child in this way:

> "I felt closer to the idea of a God, of a higher consciousness, and of a life force. And I sensed a continuity of the life force, of life and death. At that moment of birth, you come into contact with a greater force than yourself. And that physical experience transcends everything else."

Birth and death, intimacy and increasing separation; this is the image that we are dealing with. It is the circle of life. We see this circle manifest itself in our relationship with our children and also with our parents. We struggled to reach adulthood, and perhaps during our teenage years we fought for independence. Now we are starting the circle all over again with our own child. We begin to understand our own parents better, and suddenly realize, "Ah hah! So that's what they were trying to do!" We sense just how difficult it must have been for them. And now it is our turn, as we get into the circle as new parents. These are circles within circles, circles upon circles, each with its own endings and renewals.

During the course of your child's development there are many milestones that are repeated from your own life: learning to walk and talk, beginning school, junior high, the first date, the senior class prom, high school graduation, and finally leaving home and going off to work or college. The circle will once more return as your child marries and starts all over again with his own family. This sense of the circle was aptly described by a new father when his baby was three weeks old:

> "I am coming full circle to where my father was when I was my son's age. Now I am a parent. I am still on the circle, but in a different phase of it. A return or ending of that phase would be when my son becomes a parent—when he

leaves home, when I am no longer his caretaker, as he starts to loosen the bonds and relate to other people in the world."

There is something positive and beautiful that comes out of each change in the development of you and your child. There is never truly an ending, but rather a return and a new beginning. When you are caring for your child, you may be startled when you suddenly experience a vivid memory of your father or mother caring for you. The circle of your experiences has once more come home. Your recollection of those earlier memories and the power associated with them gives you some idea of how important this time is to your youngster, both now and in the way in which he will recall them later. And you may wish that you could protect your child from the struggles that you know lie ahead. All of these feelings are depicted in this father's words:

> "I may bend over him in the dim light and get flashes of a memory of waking up in the night in a dim room and a parent is bending over me and I think, 'God, what a different perspective.' To me it is a little moment in a day, and to him it is time standing still. He may remember that one incident, may flash back on it, for the rest of his life. Those things make me think, 'I can remember the discomforts, when I would be feeling sick and my parents would come in and nurture me,' and it makes me think I am glad I am through all of that. I am glad I am the parent, and I think about he still has to go through measles and mumps and whooping cough. He still has to go through colds and fevers. But then I think that's okay, because he does have to go through it and I don't have to go through it for him. The best thing for him is that he go through as many of these things on his own. I am there, but I am not adding the extra worry of, 'My God, Dad is worried about me.'

As you reminisce and fantasize about the future, you hope that your child will somehow be able to master those situations that you had difficulty with. You know it will be hard to resist the temptation to step in and do for your youngster. In wanting to start over, and to help your little baby lead a new life in a more positive direction than you did, the danger is that you might try to live it for him. Some parents fall into the trap of seeing the new baby as their second chance. This is, of course, his life, although you will see aspects of yourself in him no matter what you do. The growing awareness of this struggle was expressed by this new father:

> "He is going to live the life that he is going to live. And I say to myself, 'Lay off from these worries about what he's going to do and what he's not going to do.' They come from my own feelings of what I had a hard time doing. I want to live in what is the present for him. I want his future to come in daily increments, rather than try to plan it all out. But what if he would want to go to the same college I did? What a joke. It's hard to imagine, but there will probably be things I did that he will want to do, and you kind of have to be careful about what you dwell on."

At the ending of the first year, as you look back with nostalgia on your early memories, you might expect to be overwhelmed by sadness. But quite the contrary. You will find that the memories nurture you. Although on one hand you might say they are "only" memories, those past images are flowing with energy and vitality and give you something in the present, allowing you to move beyond, transcend, your fears about what lies ahead in your child's future and your concerns about your own mortality. It is as if you are telling yourself the story of your birth as a father—and you are all ears.

We can learn so much from the early period of our children's development and our responses to them. What is perhaps unique about the first year is that so many of the struggles are telescoped into such a short period of time. You're struggling to find a level of intimacy with your wife and child. You're sensitive to feeling displaced, and you want to feel that you are important to your family. You're struggling to be close to your child and yet may feel some jealousy if your wife's closeness to the baby does not also leave an opening for you. At the same time you're struggling with feelings of isolation and must also face the realities of the outside world. You know you have to be responsible, to make a decent living, so that you can provide the necessities of life for your family.

And throughout this time, even as you are trying to build a lasting rapport with your child, you also have to be able and willing to let go even though it may be difficult. This is a prominent theme, to feel hooked up and connected, engrossed, with your child and yet still see him as having his own unique personality, as being separate from you. To be available, yet to let go. These are themes that repeat themselves throughout your child's life.

In a way, we are really talking about the everlasting ebb and flow of life, which turns upon and repeats itself in a new way, with another dimension and a different perspective. As we look closely, we see the constant cycle, adding vitality and meaning to our lives. As we inch nearer to our children, we realize that we are close to the "source," to the life force itself. And there is no mistaking the energy and power that emanate here

Notes

Chapter 3: Engrossment

[1]This chapter is to a large degree based on the following research article: M. Greenberg and N. Morris, "Engrossment: The Newborn's Impact upon the Father," *American Journal of Orthopsychiatry* 44, no. 4 (1974) 520–31. © American Orthopsychiatric Association 1974.
[2]T.B. Brazelton, "What Makes a Good Father," *Redbook,* June 1970.

Chapter 4: Family Bonding

[1]M. Greenberg and N. Morris, "Engrossment: The Newborn's Impact upon the Father," *American Journal of Orthopsychiatry* 44, no. 4 (1974) 528.
[2]P. Brenner and M. Greenberg, "The Impact of Pregnancy on Marriage," *Medical Aspects of Human Sexuality* 11, no.7 (July 1977) 19.
[3]M. Greenberg, V. Vuorenkoski, T. Partanen, and J. Lind, "Behavior and Cry Patterns in the First Two Hours of Life in Early and Later Clamped Newborns," *Annales Paediatriae Fenniae* 13 (1967) 64–70.

Chapter 5: The Hospital

[1]J. Miller, "Return the Joy of Home Delivery with Fathers in the Delivery Room," *Hospital Topics,* January 1966. See also A. Colman and L. Colman, *Pregnancy: The Psychological Experience* (New York: Herder and Herder, 1971) 97.
[2]F. Leboyer, *Birth Without Violence* (New York: Alfred Knopf, 1975).
[3]See M. Greenberg, "The Father's Relationship to His Newborn in the First Week after Birth" (Unpublished manuscript, Langley Porter Psychiatric Institute Library, University of California School of Medicine, San Francisco, 1970).

[4]*Statistisch Zakboek* (Statistics Handbook), Central Bureau for Statistics, Netherlands, 1983. The percentage of home births in the Netherlands was 34.5% (1981). The infant mortality rate was 5.8 for every 1,000 live births (1982).
[5]See Health Data Summaries for California Counties, Center for Health Statistics, Department of Health Services, 1982. The infant mortality figure (1980) for Marin County, California was 7.3 per 1,000 live births. See also M. Estes, "A Home Delivery Service with Expert Consultation and Backup," *Birth and Family Journal* 5, no. 3 (1978) 151–57.
[6]See *Caesarian Childbirth,* National Institutes of Health Consensus Development Conference Summary, vol. 3, no. 6, 1980. The cesarian rate, according to this report has tripled from 5.5% in 1970 to 15.2% in 1978. The most recent 1983 statistics now show the cesarian section rate is 20.6% and may be higher in some locales. See Advance data #101, 1983 summary of National Hospital Discharge Survey, National Center for Health Statistics. Hyattsville, MD, 1983.
[7]R. Bradley, personal communication, 1980.
[8]E. Jackson et al., "A Hospital Rooming-in Unit for Four Newborn Infants and Their Mothers," *Pediatrics,* January 1948, 23–43.
[9]M. Greenberg, I. Rosenberg, and J. Lind, "First Mothers Rooming-in with Their Newborns: Its Impact on the Mother," *American Journal of Orthopsychiatry* 45, no. 5 (1973) 783–88. See also N. Shea, E. Klatskin, and E. Jackson, "Home Adjustment of Rooming-in and Nonrooming-in Mothers," *American Journal of Nursing* 52, no. 1 (1952) 65–67.
[10]M. Klaus, "The Biology of Parent to Infant Attachment," *Birth and Family Journal* 5, no. 4 (1978) 200–203.
[11]M. Greenberg, and N. Morris, "Engrossment: The Newborn's Impact on the Father," *American Journal of Orthopsychiatry* 44, no. 4 (1974) 520–31. See M. Klaus, and J. Kennell, *Parent-Infant Bonding* (St. Louis: Mosby, 1982) 57–62.
[12]M. Trause, and N. Irvin, "Care of the Sibling," in *Parent-Infant Bonding,* ed. M. Klaus and J. Kennell (St. Louis: Mosby, 1982) 126–27.
[13]M. Klaus, "Future Care of the Parents," *Birth and Family Journal* 5, no. 4 (1978) 246–48.

Chapter 7: Coming Home

[1]The scrapbook was to a large degree Claudia's idea. When Jonathan was four, he became sick enough to require hospitalization. At Claudia's suggestion, during Jonathan's hospital stay, we began taking pictures of him with many of his doctors and nurses as well as asking them to write a short note for

the scrapbook. Claudia and I were amazed how involved we all became in this process, and the hospital staff seemed equally fascinated. Often doctors, nurses, social workers, and occupational therapists would mingle about our room, wanting to look through the scrapbook, while chatting with all of us. The scrapbook gave us a sense of control in a helpless situation and allowed us to focus on our baby and his needs. It seems to me that such a scrapbook process could also be of considerable value for new parents, not only of normal babies but also of premature and ill newborns.

[2]Lind, "The Family in the Swedish Birth Room," *Birth and Family Journal* 5, no. 4 (1978) 249–51. Dr. John Lind, with whom I worked in Sweden at the Karolinska Hospital in Stockholm, was encouraging mothers as early as 1965 to attempt to get their husbands involved with the baby. To this end, he would often encourage women, even if breast feeding, to let their husbands give a bottle at the late night or early morning feeding. He felt this gave the mothers some rest as well as involving the fathers more with their babies.

[3]R. Fein, "The First Weeks of Fathering: The Importance of Choices and Supports for New Parents," *Birth and Family Journal* 3, no. 2 (1976) 53–58.

[4]There are several excellent books recently published that give guidelines to the grandparents themselves as to how they can be supportive and helpful to the new parents as well as to the new baby. These are: F. Dodson and P. Reuben, *How to Grandparent* (New York: New American Library, 1984) and L. Carter, *Congratulations: So You're Going to Be a Grandmother* (San Diego: Oak Tree Press, 1980).

Chapter 8: The Perils of Responsibility

[1]A. Holmberg, *Nomads of the Long Bow: The Siriono of Eastern Bolivia,* Publication no. 10 (Washington, D.C.: Smithsonian Institution, Institute of Social Anthropology, 1950).

[2]N. Newton and M. Mead, "Cultural Patterning of Perinatal Behavior," *Childbearing: Its Social and Psychological Aspects,* ed. S. Richardson and R. Guttmacher (New York: Williams & Wilkins, 1967).

[3]J. Clapp, personal communication, San Diego State University, May 1979. (Discussion on urbanization and origination of nonlocalized communities.)

[4]I. Bobak, personal communication and unpublished data on fathering, University of California Medical Center, School of Nursing, San Francisco, 1970.

[5]N. Tinbergen, *Social Behavior in Animals* (London: Methuen, 1953).

[6]M. Bellamy, *Encyclopedia of Sea Horses* (Hong Kong: TFH Publications, 1969).

[7]E. Merz, personal communication, Switzerland, 1975. I also observed this in Dr. Merz's collection of films of father-infant interactions among Barbary macaques.
[8]I. Devore, "Mother-Infant Reactions in Free Ranging Baboons," in *Maternal Behavior in Mammals,* ed. H. Rheingold (New York: John Wiley, 1963).
[9]T. Ransom, "Ecology and Social Behavior in Baboons (Papio Anubis) in the Gombe National Park" (Doctoral disseration, University of California, Berkeley, 1972).
[10]J. Nash, "The Father in Contemporary Culture and Current Psychologic Literature," *Child Development* 36 (1965) 261–397.
J. Howells, "Fathering," *Modern Perspectives in International Child Psychiatry,* vol. 3, ed. J. Howells (Edinburgh: Oliver & Boyd, 1969).
[11]I. Josselyn, "Cultural Forces, Motherliness and Fatherliness," *American Journal of Orthopsychiatry* 26 (1956) 264.
[12]There are now increasing numbers of researchers who describe the father's contribution in his child's development as well as the unique ways in which fathers relate to infants. These researchers include M. Kotelchuck, Michael Yogman, T. Berry Brazelton, Ross Parke, David Lynn, Michael Lamb, James Herzog, and Henry Biller. Some excellent reviews of their work are D. Lynn, *The Father: His Role in Child Development* (Monterey, CA, Brooks-Cole, 1974); F. Earls, "The Fathers (Not the Mothers): Their Importance and Influence with Infants and Young Children," *Psychiatry* 39 (1975) 209–25; M. Lamb, *The Role of the Father in Child Development* (New York: Wiley, 1976); S. Cath, A. Gurwitt, and J. Ross, *Father and Child: Developmental and Clinical Perspectives* (Boston: Little Brown, 1982).
[13]J. Bowlby, personal communication, Tavistock Clinic, London, October 1975, in a discussion on bonding and fathering. Dr. John Bowlby lends some credence to these ideas by commenting on the existence of attachment behaviors among fathers and babies, stating it is likely that it is only a matter ot time before a biological basis for father attachment is proven conclusively.

Chapter 9: The Tyranny of Crying

[1]A. Thomas, S. Chess, et al., *Behavioral Individuality in Early Childhood* (New York: New York University Press, 1971).
[2]P. Ostwald, *Soundmaking: The Acoustic Communication of Emotion* (Springfield, IL: Charles C. Thomas, 1968) 39.
[3]R.S. Illingworth, *The Normal Child: Some Problems of the Early Years and Their Treatment* (Edinburgh: Churchill Livingston, 1983) 272.
[4]B. Spock, *Baby and Child Care* (New York: Simon & Schuster, 1977).
[5]J. Welsh, personal communication, 1984.

[6]J. Welsh, personal communication, 1984. Dr. John Welsh, a pediatrician with over thirty years of clinical practice in San Diego has found that parents, by themselves, stumble on a variety of ways to cope with their infant's cries.
[7]G. Nelson, Presentation on bonding at a conference on "Prevention of Child Abuse," sponsored by Family Stress Center, San Diego, CA, May 1978. See also G. Nelson, *The One Minute Scolding* (Boulder, CO: Shambhala Publications, 1984).

Chapter 10: Jealousy

[1]P. Brenner and M. Greenberg, "The Impact of Pregnancy on Marriage," *Medical Aspects of Human Sexuality* 11, no. 7 (July 1977) 15–20.
[2]M. Greenberg and P. Brenner, "The Newborn's Impact on Parents' Marital and Sexual Relationship," *Medical Aspects of Human Sexuality* 11, no. 8 (August 1977) 16–28.
[3]N. Newton and M. Mead, "Cultural Patterning of Perinatal Behavior." *Childbearing—Its Social and Psychological Aspects,* ed. S. Richardson and A. Guttmacher (New York: Williams & Wilkins, 1967).
[4]N. Fock, "South American Birth Customs in Theory and Practice." *Cross-cultural Approaches: Readings in Comparative Research,* ed. C. S. Ford (New Haven: Human Relations Area Files Press, 1967).
[5]B. Blackwood, *Both Sides of Baker Passage* (Oxford: Clarendon Press, 1935).

Chapter 12: Recharging Your Parenting Battery

[1]P. Brenner and M. Greenberg, "The Impact of Pregnancy on Marriage," *Medical Aspects of Human Sexuality* 11, no. 7 (July 1977) 15–20.
[2]See E. Bing and L. Colman, *Making Love During Pregnancy* (New York: Bantam Books, 1977) 133–55. This book has an excellent chapter on sexuality in the postpartum period.
[3]W. Masters and V. Johnson, *Human Sexual Response* (Boston: Little Brown, 1966). See also C. Falicov, "Sexual Adjustment during First Pregnancy and Postpartum," *American Journal of Obstetrics and Gynecology* 117, no. 7 (December 1973) 991–1000.
[4]M. Greenberg and P. Brenner, "The Newborn's Impact on Parents' Marital and Sexual Relationship," *Medical Aspects of Human Sexuality* 11 no. 8 (August 1977) 16–28. Much of the material in this section is based upon this reference.

Chapter 13: Sharing

[1]J. Bowlby, *Attachment and Loss,* Volume 1, *Attachment* (New York: Basic Books, 1969). See also J.A. Ambrose, "The Smiling and Related Responses in Early Human Infancy: An Experimental and Theoretical Study of Their Course and Significance" (Ph.D. thesis, University of London, 1960).
[2]T.B. Brazelton, "What Makes a Good Father," *Redbook,* June 1970.
[3]M. Greenberg, and N. Morris, "Engrossment: The Newborn's Impact upon the Father," *American Journal of Orthopsychiatry,* 44, no. 4 (1974) 520–31.
[4]M. Lamb, "Infants, Fathers and Mothers: Interaction at Eight Months of Age at the Home and in the Laboratory," Proc. meeting of Eastern Psychological Association, 1975.
[5]T.B. Brazelton, "Future Care of the Infant," *Birth and Family Journal* 5, no. 4 (1978) 242–45. See also M.E. Lamb, "Infant Attachment to Mothers and Fathers," Proc. meeting Soc. Res. in Child Development, 1975.
[6]J. Nash, "The Father in Contemporary Culture and Current Psychological Literature," *Child Development* 36 (1965) 261–97.

Chapter 14: Holding Time

[1]J. Trost, "Parental Benefits—A Study of Men's Behavior and Views, Current Sweden." The Swedish Institute, Stockholm, Sweden, June 1983. See also R. Fein, "The First Weeks of Fathering: The Importance of Choices and Supports for New Parents," *Birth and Family Journal* 3, no. 2. (1976) 53–57.
[2]M. Greenberg, "The Father's Relationship to His Newborn in the First Week After Birth" (Unpublished manuscript, Langley Porter Psychiatric Institute Library, University of California School of Medicine, San Francisco, 1970).

Chapter 15: Portapouch and Backpack

[1]K. Ditella and J. Lind, "Baby Carriers in Bolivia and Sweden," *Birth and Family Journal* 4, no. 3 (1977) 123–25.

Chapter 16: Secret Weapons

[1]It will be important to discuss the crying difficulties of your baby with your pediatrician. Discuss with him your approach and ask for his recommendation. Before you decide to swaddle, consult your pediatrician.

Chapter 17: A Chapter for Mothers

[1]C. Barnett, P. Leiderman, R. Grobstein, and M. Klaus, "Neonatal Separation: The Maternal Side of Interactional Deprivation," *Pediatrics* 45 (1970) 197–205.
[2]M. Westmoreland, personal communication, 1970.
[3]J. Kennell, H. Slyter, and M. Klaus, "The Mourning Response of Parents to the Death of a Newborn Infant," *New England Journal of Medicine* 283 (1970) 344–49.
[4]M. Mead, Public lecture at University of California at San Diego, 1972.
[5]U. Bronfenbrenner and S. Byrne, "Nobody Home: The Erosion of the American Family," *Psychology Today,* May 1977, 41–47.
[6]G. Peterson, L. Mehl, and P.H. Leiderman, "The Role of Some Birth-related Variables in Father Attachment," *American Journal of Orthopsychiatry* 49, no. 2, 330–38.

Chapter 18: Spelling

[1]I. Yalom, D. Lunde, R. Moos, and D. Hamburg, " 'Postpartum Blues' Syndrome, a Description and Related Variables," *Arch. Gen. Psychiatry* 18, no. 1 (January 1968) 16–27.
[2]E. Neumann, *The Great Mother: An Analysis of the Archetype* (Princeton, N.J.: Princeton University Press, 1972) 94–119.
C.G. Jung et al., *Man and His Symbols* (Garden City, N.Y.: Doubleday, 1968) 67–82. See also "Psychological Aspects of the Mother Archetype," in *The Collected Works of C.G. Jung,* Vol. 9, part 1 (Princeton, N.J.: Princeton University Press, 1971) 75–110.
[3]A. Yates, "Narcissistic Traits in Certain Abused Children," *American Journal of Orthopsychiatry* 51, no. 1 (1981) 55–62.